Manage Stress

Take back control in your life

JAMES MANKTELOW

LONDON, NEW YORK,
MUNICH, MELBOURNE, DELHI

Produced for Dorling Kindersley
by **terry jeavons**&**company**

Project Editor · Fiona Biggs
Project Art Editor · Terry Jeavons
Designer · JC Lanaway

Senior Editor · Simon Tuite
Senior Art Editor · Sara Robin
DTP Designer · Traci Salter
Production Controller · Stuart Masheter

Executive Managing Editor · Adèle Hayward
Managing Art Editor · Nick Harris

Art Director · Peter Luff
Publisher · Corinne Roberts

Special Photography · Mike Hemsley

First published in 2007 by Dorling Kindersley Limited
80 Strand, London, WC2R 0RL
The Penguin Group
2 4 6 8 10 9 7 5 3 1
Copyright © 2007 Dorling Kindersley Limited
Text copyright © 2007 James Manktelow

A CIP catalogue record for this book is
available from the British Library
ISBN-978-1-40531-755-9

ED255
Printed and bound in China by Leo Paper Group

Contents

1 Understand Stress

2 Manage Job Stress

Introduction

Stress can make your working life miserable. However, with a little knowledge and understanding, you can learn to calm your stress and turn seemingly unpleasant jobs into satisfying and rewarding ones.

Almost everyone, at some point in life, has had that terrible feeling of being out of control at work, and has experienced that feeling of sickness in the pit of the stomach during difficult and unpleasant situations. In your case, perhaps there's far too much work to do, and too little time in which to do it. Perhaps you're up against a series of punishing deadlines, or you're being pressurized to do a job that would tax super-human abilities. Maybe a job or career you once relished has turned into a daily grind.

You need never allow stress to get the better of you

Perhaps the people you're working with are the problem: maybe your boss is piling on the work, your clients keep changing their minds, or your co-workers seem more interested in playing politics than they are in doing the job.

In some situations (and with a little extra understanding) you can change things to relieve stress. In others, you can do a lot to improve things by changing the way you look at problems. In still others, you can learn to survive stress better, partly by using relaxation techniques and partly by getting the help and support you need when you need it.

Manage Stress will help you to spot where you can take action to change things. It gives you the tools and the techniques you need to take stress out of your environment, rebalance your workload, refocus your life and career, and break through the obstacles standing in your way.

It will help you to deal better with your boss, manage and neutralize office politics, work with colleagues, reduce adrenalin levels, and perform successfully under pressure.

You will see how to take a fresh look at situations so that you can find the good in them, you will learn to manage the cycles of negative thinking that can bring unhappiness, and when you can't do anything to change a bad situation, you will be able to draw effectively on help and support.

Self-Assessment

This questionnaire will help you to reflect on your current experience of stress so that you can start thinking about how to change your life for the better. Complete the questionnaire before you read the book, and again afterwards. You should see a big improvement in the quality of your life the second time around!

Before **After**

1 What would you say is your current experience of stress?

- **A** It is unremitting and profoundly unpleasant.
- **B** It's intermittent – sometimes it's intense, but sometimes it's not an issue.
- **C** It's occasional, but is not usually a problem.

2 How do you approach major changes?

- **A** I often rush into things without much thought.
- **B** I sometimes hold back when I'm feeling stressed.
- **C** I think about long-term stress levels before I make any new commitments.

3 How would you rate your working environment?

- **A** It's generally chaotic and unpleasant.
- **B** It would benefit from some improvement.
- **C** It's fine – I find it pleasant and conducive to work.

4 What happened when you last discussed your performance with your manager?

- **A** My manager doesn't give feedback.
- **B** The feedback didn't seem to fit the job I'm doing.
- **C** I was told that I was progressing steadily towards the objectives we'd agreed.

5 **What was your workload like during the last couple of weeks?**

A I worked late several times, but even then I left a lot of work undone.

B I did quite a lot of "out of hours" work.

C My workload has been reasonably well under control.

6 **When you have too much work on, what do you do?**

A I frequently work late to get on top of it.

B I try to get someone to help me with it.

C I make sure that I get the help I need when I need it.

7 **How would you describe your manager?**

A Generally demanding and ruthless.

B Sometimes fair, sometimes pushy.

C My manager works hard to help me to do a good job.

8 **How helpful are your co-workers?**

A They're not. What's worse, I feel completely undermined by "office politics".

B I sometimes wish people were more helpful.

C We work together reasonably well.

9 **How would you describe the team you work with?**

A It's profoundly dysfunctional.

B Sometimes it's good, sometimes it's bad.

C It's efficient and a pleasure to work with.

10 **What happens when you have to make a presentation?**

A I get so nervous that I don't perform well.

B I overcome my nerves enough to do a reasonable job.

C I use relaxation techniques to manage any adrenalin surge that I might experience.

		Before	After

11 **What do you do when you've had a particularly bad day?** *B*

- **A** I usually find that I don't sleep very well.
- **B** I find it extremely difficult to unwind.
- **C** I can let go and relax at the end of the day.

12 **What is your usual approach to forthcoming challenges at work?** *A*

- **A** I worry about all the things that could go wrong.
- **B** I wish I could be more self-confident.
- **C** I tend to approach them confidently and positively.

13 **If you get upset and angry what do you do?** *A*

- **A** I let people know how I'm feeling!
- **B** I tend to keep quiet, but sometimes I don't deal with the underlying issues.
- **C** I control myself, but where I need to, I make sure that I deal with the causes.

14 **How do you react when things are going particularly badly?** *B*

- **A** I cut myself off from people to focus on the job.
- **B** I talk about the situation with friends.
- **C** I know where to go for help, and I make sure that I ask for it when I need it.

15 **How do you feel about your job?** *B*

- **A** I've lost any passion I might have had for my work.
- **B** There are emotional rewards, but there are also many little irritations that I find difficult to deal with.
- **C** It's quite satisfying. I'm doing work I believe in.

Final Scores

	A	**B**	**C**
Before	7	8	
After			

Analysis

Mostly As

Your answers show that you're feeling very stressed. Life is difficult and unpleasant, and you may be feeling badly out of control of events. While things may look bleak now, the good news is that there's almost certainly a lot you can do to improve things. Work through this book steadily and do the exercises described. If you actually do these things (rather than just read about them) you'll find that your life gets much better! Important note: If you suspect that the stress is making you ill, or you are experiencing persistent unhappiness, make sure that you get medical help.

Mostly Bs

Your answers show that you're experiencing some stress. Things may not be really awful, although they could be a lot better. Keeping a stress diary will identify the major sources of stress in your life, and you will be able to target these with the techniques described in the book. After all, why settle for a working life that is merely acceptable when you can have a good one?

Mostly Cs

Life's going reasonably well, you're probably in a supportive environment, and you're most likely making good use of many stress management strategies. However, things change, and not all changes are for the better. Get to know the strategies and techniques described in this book so that you will be able to handle issues if they do arise. In particular, make sure that you understand and are alert to the possibility of burnout, and check yourself for the symptoms regularly.

Conclusion

If this is the first time you have done this self-assessment, then bear in mind the above analysis as you read the book. Different questions in the test are addressed by different parts of this book. As you read through the book, pay particular attention to the areas where you were experiencing particular stress, and make sure that you apply the techniques explained. Make sure you pay special attention to the points of weakness you have identified, and that you incorporate the tips and techniques into your everyday life. After you've read the book and have put these techniques into practice, have a go answering the questions in this section again. You'll almost certainly find that things have got better!

Understand Stress 1

Stress in one form or another is a part of everyday life for everyone. We may think that we understand stress, but everyone experiences stress differently, and we may not always be aware of where it comes from or how it affects us. This chapter helps you to:

- Discover what stress is and what causes it
- Understand the negative impact of stress on your health and your professional life
- Identify the sources of stress in your life
- Assess the extent to which stress affects you
- Find out how to target that stress

Manage
Stress

What Is Stress?

Stress is made up of many things. It is a family of related experiences, pathways, responses, and outcomes caused by a range of different "stressors" – the circumstances or events that cause stress.

A Lack of Control

The most commonly accepted definition of stress is that it is a condition or feeling experienced when a person perceives that "demands exceed the personal and social resources the individual is able to mobilize" (Richard S. Lazarus). When you have the time and the resources to handle a situation, you feel little stress, but when you perceive yourself as being unable to handle the demands put upon you, the stress you feel can be considerable. In this sense, stress is indeed a negative experience, but it is not an inevitable consequence of an event. The level of stress you experience depends on your perception of a situation and your real ability to cope with it.

Cope with Job Stress
Some jobs are more stressful than others. If you have a stressful job, pay particular attention to stress management.

Fight or Flight

When you experience a shock or perceive a threat, you quickly release hormones that help you to survive.

→ These hormones help you to run faster and fight harder by bringing about physiological changes, such as increasing your heart rate and raising your blood pressure, and delivering more oxygen and blood sugar to important muscles.

→ They also focus your attention on the threat, to the exclusion of almost everything else

All of this significantly improves your ability to survive life-threatening events. Unfortunately, this response will also make you excitable, anxious, jumpy, and irritable, and can reduce your ability to work effectively with other people. You will be less able to execute precise, controlled skills or make complex decisions.

Understand the Mechanisms

This definition of stress given above focuses partly on getting back in control, and partly on the way that we think about and interpret the situations in which we find ourselves. However, there are also two intertwined instinctive stress responses to unexpected events – the short-term "Fight-or-Flight" response and the long-term "General Adaptation Syndrome". The first is a basic survival instinct, while the second is a long-term effect of exposure to stress. These mechanisms can be part of the same stress response. Looking at how they can fit together will help you to identify and react to the stressors in your life in a productive manner, ensuring better results, even during the most stressful times.

Stress is what you feel when you are not in control

Understand Your Response to Stress

It is easy to think that the fight-or-flight response is triggered only by life-threatening danger, but the stressful situation does not in fact have to be all that dramatic in order to provoke the response.

It can occur when we encounter the unexpected, are frustrated or interrupted, or experience a new or challenging situation.

→ The adrenalin response is a normal part of everyday life and a part of everyday stress, although usually it has a very low intensity. In modern working life this adrenalin response is rarely of any use to us.

→ Most situations benefit from a calm, rational, controlled, and socially sensitive approach, and there are excellent techniques for keeping the fight-or-flight response to stress under control.

The General Adaptation Syndrome

Endocrinologist Hans Selye, "the father of stress", saw that many different diseases and injuries to the body seemed to cause the same symptoms in patients, and identified a general response with which the body reacts to a major stressor. He called this the General Adaptation Syndrome (GAS), which has three stages.

1 The Alarm Phase
The body reacts to the stressor.

2 The Resistance Phase
Resistance to the stressor increases as the body adapts to, and copes with it. This phase lasts for as long as the body can support this heightened resistance.

3 The Exhaustion Phase
Resistance declines substantially as the body "gives up".

G GENERAL
The alarm phase

A ADAPTATION
The resistance phase

S SYNDROME
The exhaustion phase

How Stress Can Lead to Burnout

In the business environment, exhaustion caused by stress contributes to what is often referred to as "burnout". The classic business example comes from the Wall Street trading floor, where, by most people's standards, life is stressful. Traders learn to adapt to the daily stressors of big financial decisions, and the winning and losing of large sums of money. In many cases, however, the stress increases and fatigue starts to set in. At the same time, as traders become successful and earn more and more money, their financial motivation to succeed can diminish. Ultimately, many traders experience "burnout".

What's So Threatening?

Much of the stress we experience is subtle and comes from such sources as work overload, conflicting priorities, inconsistent values, over-challenging deadlines, conflict with co-workers, and unpleasant environments. While these stressors may not actually threaten your survival, they can threaten your general wellbeing. It is important to remember that people's perception of stress is important and will determine their response to it. One person may be completely unstressed by a situation that might provoke an intense response in someone else.

Perceived Threats of Stress

Even though there are many threats that don't threaten our survival, they can still trigger the hormonal fight-or-flight response with all of its negative consequences. Stress may stem from subconsciously perceived threats to:

Our social standing

Other people's opinion of us

Our promotion prospects

Our own deeply held values

Watch Your Health

You should take stress seriously. The negative effects of stress can have a serious impact on your health, causing direct – and potentially fatal – damage to your body.

Beware of Damaging Behaviour

When under pressure, some people are more likely to drink heavily or smoke as a way of getting immediate chemical relief from stress. Others may have so much work to do that they fail to exercise or eat properly. They may cut down on sleep, or worry so much that they sleep badly. In the effort to keep up with daily work pressures, some people don't see the doctor when they need to.

Look after Your Heart

If stress is intense, and stress hormones are not "used up" by physical activity, a raised heart rate and high blood pressure can damage the arteries. When the body heals this damage, the artery walls scar and thicken, restricting the flow of blood around the body. Stress hormones then accelerate the heart to increase the blood supply to the muscles, but the blood vessels supplying the heart muscles with oxygen may have become too narrow to meet the heart's demand. If this happens to you, you may, at best, experience chest pains or, at worst, suffer a heart attack.

think SMART

!

Prevention is better than cure. The key to avoiding serious problems is to seek help before your stress reaches a level where it has become unmanageable.

If you suspect that you are prone to stress-related illness, are experiencing persistent unhappiness, or if you are in any doubt about the state of your health, you should seek appropriate medical advice immediately.

Take Regular Exercise

Whatever level of stress you are experiencing in your daily life, regular exercise should form an important part of your lifestyle. Physical activity can help by:

→ Reducing your physiological reaction to stress by eliminating the stress hormones from your system.

→ Improving your circulation, strengthening your heart, and increasing the blood supply to it, directly reducing your vulnerability to heart disease.

Take up an activity that you enjoy – that way you are more likely to keep it up. Take up running or, if you were keen on tennis when you were at school, join your local tennis club. If you're not keen on sports, start walking part of the distance to work every day or enrol in a yoga course. Start off slowly, gradually increasing the amount of time and effort you put in.

Understand the Stress–Illness Connection

Stress can impair the immune system, which explains why we are more prone to infections (including colds and flu) when we are stressed. It may exacerbate symptoms in diseases that have an autoimmune component, such as rheumatoid arthritis. It also seems to promote headaches and irritable bowel syndrome, and it is now suggested that there may be links between stress and cancer. The link between stress and heart disease is well established, and if the fight-or-flight response is triggered in someone with a damaged heart the effects could be lethal. Stress is also associated with some mental health problems, especially anxiety and acute depression.

Take stress seriously – it can damage your health

Stress and Performance

In many work situations, our stress responses can cause our performance to suffer. The best tactic is to adopt a calm, rational, controlled, and sensitive approach when dealing with difficult problems at work.

Positive Pressure

Stress can cause us to respond to situations aggressively, which can harm our social relationships, or to become passive and withdrawn, in which case we may fail to assert our rights when we should. However, the pressures and demands that may cause stress can sometimes be positive in their effect. For example, an athlete may flood his body with fight-or-flight adrenalin to power an explosive performance. Deadlines, and the pressure that they create, can push unmotivated people into action.

Case study: Coaching for Success

Manuel had just given a presentation to the board, seeking authorization for a new project. He'd been nervous beforehand – these were important people and he'd been worrying about how they'd react. He'd lost his way during the presentation several times, and had struggled to explain some of the key ideas. Worse still, the questions asked gave him the impression that people hadn't really understood what he was saying. After the presentation, his manager arranged for coaching on presentation skills and stress management. Manuel's next presentation went much better.

- *The importance of the event and the expertise of people's questions increased the pressure on Manuel to a level where it had harmed his performance.*
- *His anxieties and worries distracted him during the presentation, and each time he made a mistake he became even more distracted.*
- *The coaching Manuel's manager had arranged for him made him feel much more confident about the situation, and by using relaxation techniques he was able to calm his nerves and focus during the follow-up presentation.*

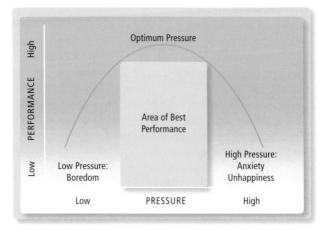

Achieve Peak Performance
This graph shows the close relationship between pressure and personal performance.

(Graph labels: PERFORMANCE — High / Low; PRESSURE — Low / High; Optimum Pressure; Area of Best Performance; Low Pressure: Boredom; High Pressure: Anxiety Unhappiness)

The "Inverted U"

The relationship between pressure and performance is very well summarized in one of the oldest and most important ideas in stress management – the "inverted-U" curve that results from plotting the pressure put on an individual against his performance of a specific task or series of tasks.

Find the Optimum Level

The graph shows that when there is very little pressure on us to carry out a task, however important it may be, there isn't a great deal of incentive for us to focus energy and attention on it, especially when there may be other, more urgent or more interesting, tasks competing for attention. As pressure on us increases, we enter the "area of best performance". Here, we are able to focus on the task and perform well – there is enough pressure to focus our attention but not so much that it actually disrupts our performance. However, as pressure increases further, there will be a dramatic decline in performance. The reasons behind this are complex – gaining an understanding of them will enable you to perform well under pressure.

The Concept of Flow

When you are operating under the level of pressure that suits you and are in your "area of best performance", you are usually able to concentrate and focus all of your attention on the important task at hand. When you are operating in this "area of best performance" without distraction, you are able to enter what Professor Mihaly Csikszentmihalyi describes as "a state of flow", where you feel "completely involved in the activity for its own sake. . . Every action, movement, and thought follows inevitably from the previous one, like playing jazz." You perform at your best "in the zone".

- You are completely absorbed in what you are doing.
- You are sufficiently motivated by what you are doing to resist competing temptations and diversions.
- You are not so stressed that anxieties and distractions interfere with your clear thinking about the task.
- You are able to focus all your efforts, resources, and abilities on the task at hand.

Achieve Flow This is an intensely creative, efficient, and satisfying state of mind. It is the state of mind in which, for example, the best speeches are made and the most impressive athletic or artistic performances are delivered.

Avoid Mental Overload

Although our brains have great processing power, we cannot be conscious of more than a few thoughts at any one time. Our "attentional capacity" is limited. When we're experiencing too much pressure or there's just too much to think about, we become uncomfortably stressed. Distractions, difficulties, anxieties, and negative thinking begin to crowd our minds, competing for our attention with the performance of the task. Our concentration suffers, and our focus narrows as the brain becomes overloaded. This creates a downward spiral – the more our brains are overloaded, the more our performance can suffer, increasing distraction and damaging performance.

Look for Alternatives

When you are stressed you can start to miss important information, and this can impair your decision-making and creativity. If you find yourself in this situation, using this knowledge can help you to avoid some of the pitfalls. If you feel highly stressed, check that you are not blindly persisting in a single course of action to the exclusion of other, possibly better, ways of proceeding.

TECHNIQUES *to* practise

You may find that being readily available to others and dealing with constantly changing information, decisions, and activities stops you achieving "flow". Periods of flow are vital to sustaining good performance, so try to find a solution that works for you.

- Let people know that you are setting aside parts of the day as quiet periods when you can work undisturbed.
- Delegate some of the activities that require the greatest levels of your concentration.
- Arrange to work from home one or two days a week.

Pinpoint the Stress in Your Life

Understanding the sources and levels of stress that affect you is an important step towards managing that stress. Learn to identify the potential causes of long- and short-term stress, and analyze your reactions to it.

Be Aware of Long-Term Stress

The first step in managing stress is understanding the stresses you experience so that you can anticipate, and prepare for, stressful situations and learn to use the stress management techniques that are most appropriate to each situation. You are probably aware of some of the immediate points of stress in your life, but you may not be as aware of the deeper, longer-term stresses.

Respond to Change

It is important to recognize that all kinds of change in your life raise your stress levels as you try to adapt. The transition from college to a new job, for example, involves radical changes in lifestyle, location, and personal status that can be deeply stressful. Anyone changing jobs, or even his or her role within the workplace, will experience a wide range of new challenges and difficulties. The joys and upsets of relationships and families also have their stresses, and all of these will have an impact on your ability to cope.

think SMART

It may be possible to manage a serious stressor by taking control of more easily manageable stressors that may be tipping the balance.

If there is a serious stressor you can't avoid, look for any addditional sources of stress. If you can take steps to control these additional stressors it will help you to bring the overall stress in your life within more manageable bounds.

Learn from Experience

Read through the three groups of life events below and make a note of how many of them apply to you.

If a large number of these life events are relevant to you, especially those in Group 3, which are the most stressful events, then you should take great care to keep your life as stable and as stress-free as you possibly can.

Schedule of Recent Experience

Group 1
- A minor violation of the law (e.g. a parking ticket or speeding fine)
- A major change in your eating or sleeping habits, in your social activities, in your usual type or amount of recreation, in the amount of participation in church activities
- Taking out a loan for a purchase such as a car, television, or freezer
- Moving house or changing to a new school
- A major change in working hours or conditions
- A revision of personal habits

Group 2
- A major change in living conditions.
- An outstanding achievement
- A son or daughter leaving home
- A major change in duties and responsibilities at work
- Foreclosure on a mortgage or loan
- Taking out a mortgage or loan for a major purchase
- A major change in the number of arguments with your partner
- Changing to a completely different line of work
- The death of a close friend
- A major change in the state of your finances
- Sexual difficulties

Group 3
- Pregnancy or gaining a new family member through adoption
- Major business re-adjustment (merger, bankruptcy), retirement from work, redundancy
- Major personal injury or illness, or health problem of a family member
- Marriage, marital reconciliation, separation, or divorce
- The death of a close family member, especially a partner or a child
- Detention in a prison or other institution

...und of your long-term stress level,
...m stress occur on a routine and daily
...clude over-demanding deadlines,
...ur co-workers, worries and anxieties, or
any or ... other possibilities. Because stress is partly
a matter of perception, and because people respond to
situations in different ways, it is important to understand
and analyze your own particular sources of stress. Keeping
a stress diary is a good way of doing this.

Use a Stress Diary

You can use a "stress diary" to record information about
the stresses you are experiencing, so that you can analyze
these stresses – which rarely receive the attention they
deserve – and determine how best to prevent them or
deal with them effectively and efficiently.

Stress Diary

Date/time	Event	Stress experienced	Scale 1–10
08/03 9.45	Argument with MM	High	9
08/03 11.00	Worrying about deadline	Moderate	4
08/03 16.30	Backache	Low	3

Record Your Stress If you learn to
identify recurring stresses you will be
able to do something about controlling
your reaction to them.

TECHNIQUES
to practise

Record stressful events on a daily basis, detailing the nature of each event, and why it caused stress. Also record, on a scale of 1–10, the level of stress you experienced and how it made you feel. You can also record how you dealt with the stressful situation. Gathering information regularly and routinely over a period of time about the stress you are experiencing will help you to separate the more common, routine stresses from those that occur only occasionally. It will also give you an important insight into how you react to stress, help you to identify the level of stress at which you prefer to operate, and show whether your reactions are appropriate and useful.

- Make entries in your stress diary at fixed points during the day, for example every hour, or every three hours.
- If you tend to forget to do this set an alarm to remind you when you should be making your next diary entry.
- Make a diary entry only if an incident is stressful enough for you to feel that it is significant.

Analyze the Information

By keeping a stress diary you can uncover patterns of stress and extract the information you need about the stressful events and situations in your life. When you have been keeping your stress diary for a month, list the different stresses you experienced during this time by frequency, with the most frequent kind of stress at the top of the list. Then prepare a second list that ranks all the stressful experiences by how bad they made you feel, with the most unpleasant stresses at the top of the list. The stresses at the top of each list are the most important for you to learn to control. Your assessments of the underlying causes, and your appraisal of how well (or otherwise) you handled particular stressful events may reveal that you could benefit from improving your stress management skills.

Use Stress SWOT Analysis

Conventional SWOT analysis is used to look at your Strengths, Weaknesses, Opportunities, and Threats in a situation. Stress SWOT Analysis will show you where you need to improve your stress management skills.

How SWOT Works

Carrying out the Stress SWOT Analysis ensures that you recognize all the personal strengths, skills, resources, and social networks that can help you to manage stress. You may find that you have strengths and skills that you are not aware of. This analysis will highlight them. By looking at your weaknesses, you identify areas you need to change in your life, including any new skills that you need to acquire. Listing opportunities enables you see how you can take advantage of your strengths to help you manage the stress in your life, and emphasizes the rewards of good stress management. By looking at the factors that are threats, you can recognize the negative consequences of managing stress poorly, and this should be a potent source of motivation.

Seek Support

Many people become stressed because they fail to recognize the resources at their disposal and the support network on which they can draw to help them to cope with stressful situations. It is important to recognize that very few people can do everything without help. Knowing how to recognize those situations where you should draw on the help available to you is an important part of stress management.

Carry Out Your Stress SWOT Analysis

With your stress diary at hand, run through the following procedure to identify your strengths and weaknesses, your opportunities and threats, and establish how you can harness this knowledge to manage stress in your life.

1 Write down your personal **strengths**:
➔ Things you are good at and for which people respect you.
➔ People who are able to help you.
➔ The resources you can draw on.
➔ Times when you managed stress well, and the practical skills you used to do this.

2 Listing your personal **weaknesses** and the limitations of your position will help you to identify possible areas of change in your life and spot where you need to develop new skills. Write down:
➔ Areas where you are aware that you are not strong, or things that people fairly criticize you for.
➔ Any lack of resources that has an impact on your situation.
➔ Problems with your job, your relationships, your living or working environment.
➔ Times when you did not handle stress well, and why you think this was the case.

3 Think about the **opportunities** that are available to you:
➔ Work your way through your strengths, and ask yourself how you can draw on these strengths to help you to manage stress.
➔ Work through your weaknesses. Identify opportunities for positive change and the development of new skills.
➔ Consider the practical opportunities that would be open to you if you were to take advantage of these opportunities to improve your stress management.

4 When considering your **threats**, think about the consequences of leaving your weaknesses uncovered, and about the damage to your relationships, career, and happiness that would result. Use this consideration of the downside as a spur to ensure that you take stress management seriously in the future!

Summary: Sources of Stress

In order to deal effectively with the stress in your life, it is important to understand precisely where the stress you experience comes from, to analyze your reactions to it, and work to improve your responses. You can then anticipate stressful situations, prepare for them, and learn to use the most appropriate stress management techniques.

Understanding Your Stress

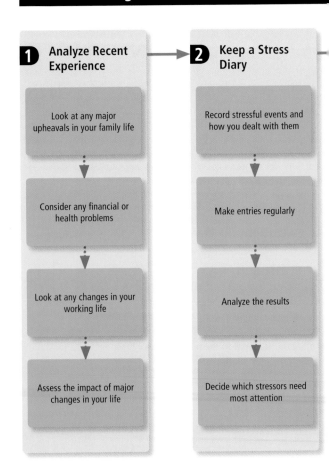

1 Analyze Recent Experience

Look at any major upheavals in your family life

Consider any financial or health problems

Look at any changes in your working life

Assess the impact of major changes in your life

2 Keep a Stress Diary

Record stressful events and how you dealt with them

Make entries regularly

Analyze the results

Decide which stressors need most attention

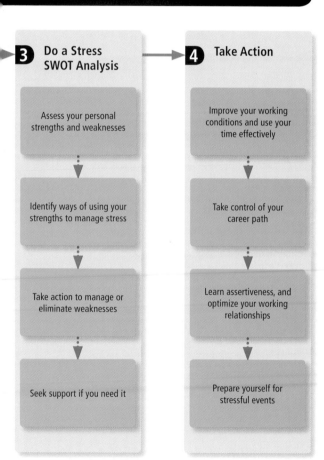

3 Do a Stress SWOT Analysis

Assess your personal strengths and weaknesses

↓

Identify ways of using your strengths to manage stress

↓

Take action to manage or eliminate weaknesses

↓

Seek support if you need it

4 Take Action

Improve your working conditions and use your time effectively

↓

Take control of your career path

↓

Learn assertiveness, and optimize your working relationships

↓

Prepare yourself for stressful events

Target Your Stress Effectively

So far you have looked at what stress is, and at how it affects your health and your performance. If you can work out how to manage the stresses that your career brings, you will be able to rise above them.

Prioritize Your Stresses

Once you have identified the main sources of stress in your life, the next step is to prioritize them so that you can separate the more important stressors from the minor, infrequent irritations that do not deserve much attention.

- Work through your Schedule of Recent Experience sheet and list the events that still cause you stress now.
- Look at the two lists you prepared during the analysis of your stress diary. The first of these showed the most frequent things that caused you stress, while the second list showed the most unpleasant ones. Add these things to your list.
- Run through the list of weaknesses and threats that you identified in your Stress SWOT Analysis. If any of these cause some of the stress that you are currently experiencing, make a note of them.
- Consolidate any items that have the same underlying cause so that each source of stress

Identify Major Stressors

Schedule of Recent Experience

⇩

Stress Diary

⇩

Stress SWOT Analysis

⇩

Consolidation

⇩

Ranking of Stressors

Learn to Manage Stress

Once you have identified the most important sources of stress in your life, the next step is to identify stress management techniques that will help you to deal with them. There are three major approaches to this:

→ **Action-oriented approaches** – These confront the problem causing the stress, and change the environment or the situation. When you have some power in a situation, action-oriented approaches are some of the most satisfying and rewarding ways of managing stress.

→ **Emotionally-oriented approaches** – When you do not have the power to change the situation, you can try to manage your stress by changing your interpretation of the situation and the way you feel about it.

→ **Acceptance-oriented approaches** – When something has happened over which you have no power and no emotional control (for example, when a loved one dies), your focus is on surviving the stress. You need to build buffers to help you to survive situations that you cannot change, and learn to cope with the long-term stress that can lead to burnout.

appears only once on the list. Strike out those that you do not expect to happen again, or that are so minor that you would not normally worry about them.
- Rank the remaining items with the most important stressors at the top of the list and the least important at the bottom. The items at the top of the list are those that are most important for you to resolve.

TIP Put together your list of stressors using a spreadsheet on your computer – the list will then be much easier to sort into the correct order.

Manage
Job Stress

2

People within successful organizations will often become very successful themselves, but the price of this success is often stress. There are also more subtle stresses that come from inconsistent and conflicting priorities and demands, and a lack of obvious career prospects. This chapter shows you how to:

- Improve your journey to work, and your working conditions
- Analyze your job to arrive at a better understanding of your priorities
- Negotiate the time and resources you need
- Plan tasks and projects in a way that minimizes stress
- Plan your career and break through blocks
- Survive an intrinsically stressful job

Control Environmental Stress

You experience a variety of small environmental stresses every day, from the frustrations of commuting to badly organized work spaces. However, with a little planning, many of these stresses can be controlled quite easily.

Recognize How It All Adds Up

Everyday annoyances can be very small and seem minor – a traffic jam, a backache caused by sitting in a badly designed or uncomfortable chair, the distraction of some gossiping colleagues, a lost document in a cluttered office – but each one can trigger a small release of stress hormones into your body and this will affect your overall sense of wellbeing. If you can take steps to control the background level of stress you should be able to reduce the impact of the major stressors when they occur.

Case study: Analyzing Your Job

Katrina's job was very unpredictable and whenever something went wrong, she was the one who had to sort it out. Realizing that her job was a stressful one, she did what she could to balance this stress. She played relaxing music in her car during her long commute, reorganized the layout of her office to make it as efficient as possible, purchased plants, and brought in daylight lighting. While she still had a stressful job, these actions reduced her overall stress.

• By thinking about her commute Katrina was able to take steps to reduce the stress it caused.
• By reorganizing her office space and improving her working environment, she eliminated many of the small irritations that were contributing to her stress.
• By changing her work environment to make it as pleasant and enjoyable as she could, Katrina gave herself something pleasant to enjoy when she was feeling down.

TIP When you have recognized the imperfections of your environment, change what you can, and try to see the rest as necessary costs with positive benefits.

To reduce the stress caused by commuting you can learn to maximize your control, minimize your discomfort, and remain calm and collected.

Consider some of the following techniques to reduce commuting stress.

- Leave earlier for work and beat the rush.
- Find a better way around regular congestion spots.
- Adjust the controls of your car so the driving position is as comfortable as possible.
- Play calming music whenever you feel frustrated by delays and difficulties.
- Use your positive thinking skills to think about your commute in a more positive and resourceful way.
- When using public transport, read a book or magazine or distract yourself in some way.

On the Way to Work

However it is done, commuting can be a source of unpleasant stress. If you commute by car, you can experience stress from traffic congestion, physical discomfort, air pollution, and noise. Congestion is often the most intense source of frustration – your goal is to get to work or home as quickly as possible, and congestion directly prevents you from achieving this, taking away your control. Commuting by public transport has its own set of stresses – the lack of control over your environment, overcrowding, violation of personal space, noise, delay, and unwelcome interaction with other travellers.

Move Further Out

The stresses of public transport are more difficult to manage than car commutes because you have less control over the situation. A long-term solution may be to move closer to the start of a commuting route where crowding is usually less intense, giving you the chance to find a seat and the freedom to arrange yourself and your possessions.

Improve Your Office

The conditions in which you work can have a major impact on the way you feel about your job, and the layout of your working space is of paramount importance. People and resources need to be immediately at hand if you are to work efficiently. An open plan environment can promote good communication and team performance, but the noise of office equipment, telephones, and people talking can be immensely distracting. If this is a source of stress, try using furniture, screens, blinds, and plants to create personal space and muffle distracting noise.

A pleasant environment reduces stress levels

Make Yourself Comfortable

Badly designed and uncomfortable furniture, the incorrect positioning of computer equipment, inadequate lighting, poor air quality, thoughtless office planning and cramped, inadequate work spaces – all of these can add to everyday tensions and frustrations by causing backache, eye strain, dry throat, headaches, fatigue, and a host of other niggling discomforts. All of the things that cause these problems can be solved with a little thought and expenditure, and the benefits are well worth the cost.

think SMART

The simple process of pinpointing and making a note of your everyday stressors can help to make them much more manageable.

At the end of the day, look at these things and think what you can do about them. Where you can, take action to manage each of the problem factors to make life more comfortable.

Brighten Up

In the scale of all business expenses, it doesn't cost much to keep your work space up to a reasonable standard and to make it a pleasant place in which to work, reducing stress and increasing efficiency.

Use Light and Plants

Most people like bright daylight, so consider fitting broad spectrum lighting. Position your computer screen in such a way that glare from natural or artificial light is eliminated. Keeping plants in your office can have a calming influence – take the time to nurture them as a neglected plant can instill feelings of guilt.

Be Ergonomic

Arrange your working environment so that it is comfortable, making sure that your seat is properly adjusted and that the computer monitor and keyboard are comfortably placed.

Create Mental Space

Use partitioning to create a quiet oasis in which you can better concentrate. Photos and pictures will personalize your work space and improve your sense of wellbeing while at work.

TIP Take regular breaks away from your desk in order to clear your mind and reenergize your body.

Analyze Your Job

To do a good job, you need to know what is expected of you. While this may seem obvious, in the hurly-burly of a new, fast-moving, high-pressure role, it is something that is often overlooked in order to get the job done.

Find Out What Matters

Job analysis is a useful technique for getting a firm grip on what really is important in your job. By understanding the priorities in your job and identifying what constitutes success, you can focus on these activities and minimize work on other tasks. This gives you the greatest return from the work you do, keeping your workload under control and reducing the stress factors.

Understand Your Organization's Goals

Your job will exist for a reason, and this will be determined by the strategy of the unit you work for. This is often expressed in a mission statement and, in some way, what you do should help the organization achieve its mission. (If it does not, you have to ask yourself how secure your job is!) Look at which of your objectives contribute towards the mission. These should be the major objectives of your job. If they are not, make a note of this.

Use Winning Ways

HIGH IMPACT

- Knowing your job priorities
- Focusing clearly on your performance measures
- Contributing creatively to your team's "mission"
- Getting good, job-focused training in key areas
- Taking the lead from high achievers by copying them

NEGATIVE IMPACT

- Failing to prioritize work
- Ignoring performance measures
- Refusing to plan ahead
- Assuming that appropriate training will come your way if you wait long enough for it
- Allowing others to look after your career instead of progressing it yourself

Understand the Organizational Culture

Every organization has its own culture – historically developed values, rights and wrongs, and things that it considers to be important. If you are new to the job, talk with established, respected members of staff to understand these values. Ask yourself how your job objectives fit with these values. Do they reinforce the organization's culture, or clash with it? If looked at through the lens of the organizational culture, would the job you do be valued by your organization?

Know What Your Priorities Are

Knowing what to concentrate on will help you to perform well and minimize stress. It may seem like a very basic requirement that you should know what the priorities of your job are, but many people, when asked, can give only the vaguest of answers. If you don't have a clear job description, or if you report to more than one person in the department or organization, you may find that competing demands on your time and resources are causing you to experience high levels of stress.

If your job description hasn't been updated as you've progressed through the organization, it can help you to identify and focus on the priorities of your job if you write a job description for yourself.

• Make a comprehensive list of the activities in which you are currently engaged in the course of your day-to-day activities.

• Add anything that you think you should be doing and that you have identified as something that will advance you in your long-term objective of advancing your career within the organization.

• Delete from the list any activity that you believe is squandering your talents and that could be done by someone else in the organization.

• Discuss your list with your manager and suggest that it could be used as the basis for an up-to-date job description.

Understand Top Achievers

Find out who the top achievers are and why they are successful. Inside or outside the organization, there may be people in a similar role to you who are seen as highly successful. Find out how they work and what they do to generate this success. Learn their skills and approaches.

Understand Your Career Prospects

Sometimes jobs are created to solve a particular problem and little thought is given to career progression. These can be dead-end jobs that can harm you career if you stay in them too long. If little thought has been put into the design of your current job, you could find that career progression from this position may not be a possibility. You need to work to ensure that you are sensibly placed for your next career move, and, if the next move is not obvious, this may be a matter of serious concern. Even if a job seems very attractive, ask the right questions about career progression before accepting it.

> **Being able to handle stress is perhaps the most basic of job expectations; it is at the core of not just doing good work but doing work, period.**
>
> Cora Daniels

Confirm Your Job Priorities

By this stage, you should have a good understanding of what your job entails, and what your key objectives are. You should also have a good assessment of any lack of clarity in objectives, any lack of resource, and any discrepancies or inconsistencies between what you believe your job to be and the realities of the situation. Any of these could potentially undermine you in your role, thereby causing you stress. Talk these through with your manager, and make sure that you resolve them in a satisfactory way.

Case study: Analyzing Your Job

Clarissa was very upset. Despite working harder than ever, she couldn't get on with her new manager. Suspecting that something structural was wrong, she conducted a job analysis exercise. Working through her old job description, she saw that the job she was doing now had moved on. While she was a key member of her team, her work did not contribute directly to the measurable goals of the department and didn't match the vision her new manager had recently explained. They discussed this together, and, with a little negotiation, things were soon going well. Clarissa's job description was seriously out of date. The company's direction had changed, while Clarissa's role, responsibilities, and goals had not.

- *By renegotiating her job with her new manager, Clarissa was able to drop many old duties, and refocus her efforts on activities that were regarded by the organization as more important. This made her workload much more manageable.*
- *Her manager understood more about what she was doing, and became more flexible in her expectations of Clarissa.*

Create More Time

People often create great stress by underestimating the length of time activities will take to complete. Improving your time estimation skills will help you to handle a highly demanding and potentially stressful workload.

Take Control

Time management helps you to reduce long-term stress by giving you direction when you have too much work to do. It puts you in control of where you are going, and helps you to increase your productivity. By eliminating time-wasting and low-yield activities you will be making the best use of your time, you will enjoy your current role more, and will find that you are able to allocate more time to relaxing outside work and enjoying life. Being disciplined in your approach to your working life will reduce your stress levels.

Prioritize Interruptions Assess the person interrupting you and what it is they are asking. If one or both are important to you it makes sense to say yes; otherwise, learn to say no.

5 minute FIX

Others may be unaware that they are adding to your stress. Don't just say "yes" when you're already overloaded.

- Prepare some polite but assertive ways of turning the extra work away.
- Negotiate to defer or reprioritize work for the person asking.
- Ask for some extra resources or time to carry out the work.

TECHNIQUES
to practise

In order to know how productively you are using your time, you need to know just how much your time is worth.

If you are in the employment of someone else, it is important to understand how much your employer is paying for your time and the resources you use, and how much profit you are expected to generate. If you are working for yourself, you should have a good idea of how much income you need to cover the expenditure of your time.

- Work these figures back to an hourly rate.
- Looking at your workload, estimate the value to the organization of each task you perform.
- Using your hourly rate, work out the rough cost of each task you carry out.
- Where you have a choice, concentrate on tasks with a value greater than the calculated value of your time.
- Whenever possible, eliminate or delegate tasks that have a lower value than your time.

Assess How You Spend Your Time

An activity log, in which you simply record what you are doing throughout the day, is an important tool for reviewing your use of time. It helps you to understand how you use your time, so that you can identify and eliminate time-wasting and unproductive habits. This gives you more time to do your work and increases your efficiency, making it more likely that you will be able to leave work on time and have good quality time to yourself to relax. When you start keeping your log you will probably be surprised at how much time you waste every day. Eliminating any unproductive activities will put you back in control.

TIP Cutting out time wasting often involves saying "No" to people. Whenever you have to do this, be courteous and explain why.

Compile and Use Your To Do List

When problems seem overwhelming, or there is a huge number of demands on your time, keeping a to do list will help you to establish priorities and gives you a starting point for negotiating deadlines.

Establishing priorities will make your workload more manageable and will reduce your stress, so write down a complete list of all the tasks that face you now.

→ Break down large tasks into their component elements. If these still seem large, break them down again. Do this until all tasks are shown as manageable pieces of work.

→ Run through the tasks and allocate priorities from A (very important) to F (unimportant). Base your assessment of priority on the criteria of urgency and importance.

→ Consider the results of your job analysis when prioritizing your list. Tasks that contribute to your job objectives should rank as high priority.

→ If too many tasks have a high priority ranking, run through the list again and demote the less important ones. Once you have done this, rewrite the list in order of priority.

→ Now, work your way through the tasks on your list in order of priority. By doing this, you will do the most important jobs first and will therefore make the best use of your time.

Create a To Do List

Break down tasks
▽
Allocate priorities
▽
Assess job analysis results
▽
Rewrite the list in order of priority
▽
Work through the tasks in order

Activity Log

Date	Activity	Duration
11/02	Making coffee	5 minutes
11/02	Opening and reading mail	35 minutes
11/02	Reading industry press	40 minutes

Analyze Your Activity Log

Every time you change activities, note the activity's duration. You may decide to integrate your activity log with your stress diary. Do this for several days and then analyze the log. You may be alarmed to see the amount of time you spend doing low value jobs such as reading direct mail or newspapers, browsing interesting but unhelpful web pages, talking to colleagues, waiting for meetings to begin, travelling, etc.

Keep a Log Using a template like the one shown here, make a note of all the things you do each day, as you do them.

Use a To Do List

Once you know which tasks are most valuable, and which time-wasting activities can be eliminated, you can organize and prioritize your workload to ensure that you concentrate on the most important, highest-yield work. Keeping a to do list is a basic working skill that helps you to deliver work reliably, without letting tasks "slip through the cracks". This obviously helps in reducing the stress that rightly comes from failing to do something important!

> **In corporate America, especially, people often rise to the top by learning how to overcome stress.**
>
> Cora Daniels

Meet Your Deadlines

If your jobs have high visibility, must be completed to a deadline, or involve co-ordinating several people to achieve a single goal, you will need a planning tool that is more powerful than your to do list.

Develop an Action Plan

The use of an action plan can help you to make a credible assessment of the amount of time you'll need to manage a medium-sized project with a reasonable deadline.

- Write down all the tasks for the project in the order in which they need to be completed.
- Estimate the duration of each task and add a contingency to allow for any time lost.
- Calculate how long the plan will take to complete.

This sequential task list will also show you what resources you will need for each task and when you will need them. You can now work out a realistic delivery time, helping you to develop a reputation for reliability while shielding yourself from deadline stress.

Delegate Tasks

If you are successful in your career, the demands on you will soon become greater than you are able to cope with on your own. As you approach this point, you will find your stress levels rising. If your role up to now has been very hands on, you may find it difficult to hand over jobs that you know you can do. Delegation is the skill that you must acquire to manage this work and to ensure that it is delivered.

Plan Ahead

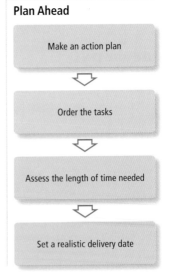

Make an action plan

▽

Order the tasks

▽

Assess the length of time needed

▽

Set a realistic delivery date

Decide What to Delegate

Work through your action plan and see whether there are any tasks that can be delegated to someone who is not as overloaded as you and who can help you.

Find the Right Person

Look for someone who is capable and willing to do the work, and who has the time to do it properly. Brief her fully, telling her:

- Why the job needs to be done, and how this will help the client, the organization, or the team.
- What needs to be done and what has to be delivered.
- The resources that are available and the constraints within which the work will need to be carried out.
- The date by which the work needs to be completed.
- That you will be available to give information or coaching where needed.
- The checkpoints during the project at which you will review progress.

Then let go (until the first checkpoint)!

5 minute FIX

If your action plan shows that you won't make your deadline, take five minutes to look at your strategy.

- Find out whether more resources are available to speed up the work.
- Delegate some of the essential tasks.
- Propose a revised delivery date. Don't let people down at the last minute.

Delegate Successfully

HIGH IMPACT

- Delegating tasks on the basis of people's ability to do them
- Monitoring at regular, agreed checkpoints someone who is performing a delegated task
- Showing your appreciation

NEGATIVE IMPACT

- Retaining the best tasks and delegating the worst
- Refusing to allow people to perform the delegated tasks in their own way
- Failing to appreciate effort

Summary: Maximizing Efficiency

Work overload is a common source of workplace stress. You can take steps to deal with it by being ruthless in your use of time, accurately identifying your priorities, eliminating as many low value activities as possible, and delegating properly. Try also to eliminate uncertainty about your job and clarify your career path.

Getting the Job Done

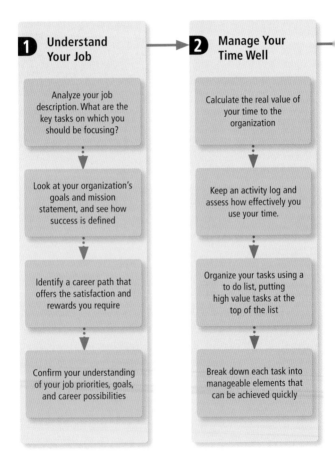

1 Understand Your Job

Analyze your job description. What are the key tasks on which you should be focusing?

Look at your organization's goals and mission statement, and see how success is defined

Identify a career path that offers the satisfaction and rewards you require

Confirm your understanding of your job priorities, goals, and career possibilities

2 Manage Your Time Well

Calculate the real value of your time to the organization

Keep an activity log and assess how effectively you use your time.

Organize your tasks using a to do list, putting high value tasks at the top of the list

Break down each task into manageable elements that can be achieved quickly

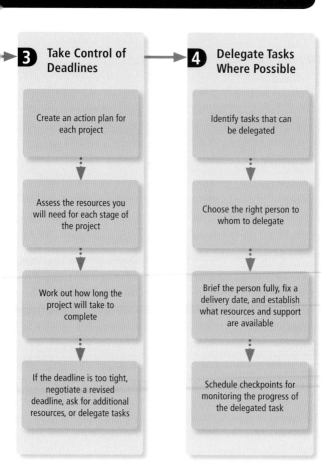

▶ **3**	**Take Control of Deadlines**	▶	**4**	**Delegate Tasks Where Possible**

| Create an action plan for each project | | | Identify tasks that can be delegated |

| Assess the resources you will need for each stage of the project | | | Choose the right person to whom to delegate |

| Work out how long the project will take to complete | | | Brief the person fully, fix a delivery date, and establish what resources and support are available |

| If the deadline is too tight, negotiate a revised deadline, ask for additional resources, or delegate tasks | | | Schedule checkpoints for monitoring the progress of the delegated task |

Take Control of Your Career

In the many jobs that lack established career paths, you may be the only person looking after your long-term prospects. There are several ways to avoid the stress that comes from an uncertain or stalled career future.

Avoid Stagnation

In young, fast-growing organizations, the absence of career paths is often not a problem. If you're flexible and good at what you do, opportunities will arise often, and you just need to be alert and take advantage of them. However, in more mature organizations, a lack of obvious career paths can be worrying, especially early in your career, when you need to be gaining plenty of experience as quickly as you can to qualify for better and more challenging jobs. In other organizations, it's possible to become too valuable in your job to be allowed to move forward in your career, and this, too, can be intensely frustrating.

Take Charge of Your Career Planning

If, after conducting the job analysis and talking it through with your manager, you still do not have an obvious career path open to you, you will need to take charge of your own career planning. Keep your eyes open for opportunities that present themselves.

Take Control of Your Career

Take stock

Conduct a personal inventory

Decide what you want to achieve

Identify career options

Acquire new skills or experience

Take action to progress your career

Plan Your Career Future

You need to take stock of where you are now, look at the opportunities open to you, and plan how to take advantage of those opportunities.

→ **Look at your current position** – Conduct a personal inventory of your knowledge, skills, experience, and resources.

→ **Think about your goals** – Decide what you want to achieve with your life and your career. Look at all the possibilities.

→ **Research your options** – You need to know whether the career has a future, what the requirements are to move to the next stage, and how well you will be paid as you progress.

→ **Plan your approach** – Decide what you want to achieve. If you need new skills or experience, acquire them.

→ **Take action!** – If you decide to manage your career within your current organization, start taking the necessary actions to progress your career. If you decide that you need to change organization in order to progress your career, then set about finding the best possible alternative job that you can.

Know What's Expected
Talk to people already doing the job to find out what you need to know and do to progress.

Survive a Stressful Job

Some jobs are intrinsically difficult, unpleasant, and stressful. This may be due to the nature or environment of the work itself, or because of inherent conflicts with your personal attitudes and ambitions.

Learn to Deal with the Pressure

Customer service departments in call centres can be extremely stressful, particularly when customers are demanding, unpleasant, rude, or perhaps even angry. Production line workers on continually moving production lines can experience intense pressure from the constant, unrelenting demands on their performance. Managing people can be stressful, particularly when managers are dealing with regular interruptions from staff at the same time that they are trying to complete work themselves and meet their own deadlines. Pressures and stress are part of these jobs and, while you may be able to eliminate some of them, others will always remain, and you will have to learn to deal with the stress.

Some jobs are intrinsic sources of stress

think
SMART

!

Don't burn your bridges. If you're fed up with your current situation it can be tempting to move to a completely different job in a different industry.

Think about such a move very carefully — if you're going to be successful you'll need to learn a lot about that industry and how it works. It can take a huge effort to become skilled in a completely new role, and you may experience feelings of inadequacy during the process.

Tackling a Lack of Information

The feeling of loss of control that comes from not knowing what is going on can cause severe stress, especially when people are feeling insecure about their jobs. There are several possible reasons for the lack of communication:

→ Although managers may be happy to share information, they may not always think to do so.
→ People may feel they are communicating, and be unaware that staff have misinterpreted their messages.
→ Team members may not ask for information because they are scared of their manager or are over-respectful.
→ Managers may feel it is unprofessional to pass on too much information, and therefore pass on too little.

Ask for clarification of the situation. By doing so you at least create the opportunity for more open communication.

Accept the Fixed Factors

Other major contributors to job stress are lack of information, poor environments, lack of control over work and the pace of work, frequent distractions and upsets, and frustration of goals. The demands of your job may even conflict with your own values, beliefs, or goals, and this, too, can cause intense stress.

Improve and Adapt

If your environment and working conditions are causing stress, it may be possible to improve them with very little expenditure or effort.

- If you are frequently exposed to annoying upsets and interruptions, use practical relaxation techniques to reduce the level of stress.
- If you find yourself feeling angry or negative, check whether your interpretation of the situation is accurate.

Relating Well in the Workplace

3

The people with whom you work and your relationships with them can be significant sources of stress in your work environment. Here we look at ways to reduce stress levels by examining those relationships and taking steps to ensure that they work smoothly for you. This chapter shows you how to:

- Deal constructively with people in power
- Assert your legitimate rights
- Gain support for your goals
- Cope with the unreasonable or impossible demands of others
- Review team and work structure

Deal With People in Power

There are always people who have the power to affect you and your goals. The influence of your manager, clients, politicians, and others within or outside the organization may be a source of severe stress.

Handle Potential Conflict

People may sometimes undermine or block you, load you with stressful tasks, or be unreasonable in their demands. Clients may see things in the short term and try to get as much out of you as they can, regardless of the long-term consequences for you. Your relationship with your manager is of great importance here, as you try to balance work and free time, manage your workload, and handle apparently excessive demands or unreasonable behaviour.

Case study: Setting the Limits

For months Naseema had been working long hours, trying to do all of the things her boss wanted her to do, but as soon as she finished one job, her boss would give her more to do. She was exhausted. The work was piling up around her, and she was losing sleep over it.

Reflecting on the situation, she was aware of how much she wanted to impress her manager and of how she always said "yes" politely when asked to do something. Naseema thought about what her workload should be, and arranged a meeting with her manager. She calmly and clearly explained the situation and asked for the help of an assistant. Within a month Naseema had the help she needed and was no longer losing any sleep.

• *Naseema's manager wasn't a tyrant - he was just busy himself, and assumed that Naseema would say when she was becoming overloaded.*
• *Because Naseema approached her manager in an adult way, he engaged with her as an adult and worked with her to resolve the problem she was having.*
• *By presenting a workable solution, Naseema made it easy for her manager to say "yes".*

Communicate Clearly Dealing with people in power, whether clients or managers, is all about communication. Talk over potential problems before they have a chance to get out of hand.

Believe in Yourself

If you are using time management and planning skills well, you can be confident that you are working efficiently and effectively. If you have fully clarified your job using the job analysis tool and are acting appropriately, then you are concentrating your efforts on the right activities. If your workload is still excessive or your working conditions unreasonable, you need to change the situation.

Deal with Conflict

Work efficiently to reduce the possibility of conflict

⇩

Clarify your job to reduce the possibility of excessive demands

⇩

Concentrate your efforts on effective time management

⇩

Communicate your difficulties rather than bottling them up

Resolve a Stressful Situation

This six-step procedure will help you to remedy sources of stress in an assertive way with the person in power. Use the acronym LADDER to guide you through this process.

1 Look at your rights and what you want, and understand why you feel the way you do about the situation. Analyze, as unemotionally as possible, why you feel your rights are being violated.

2 Arrange a formal meeting with the person in power to discuss the situation. This shows how important the situation is to you and ensures that sufficient time will be allocated to discussing it.

3 Define the problem specifically. Keep information objective and uncoloured by emotion. Make sure your comments are correct and are supported by the facts.

4 Describe your feelings so that the other person fully understands how you feel and how important it is to you to resolve the situation.

5 Express what you want clearly and concisely – prepare some reasonable proposals before the meeting. Be courteous, but take care not to confuse your message.

6 Reinforce your message to the other person, explaining what the benefits of the course of action will be and showing how your solution will improve the situation.

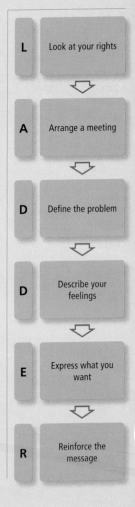

L	Look at your rights
A	Arrange a meeting
D	Define the problem
D	Describe your feelings
E	Express what you want
R	Reinforce the message

TIP If you are making a request that may be unwelcome, the best approach is to communicate your needs assertively.

Change Your Situation

You can do this well or you can do it badly. Taking a submissive position when you communicate, hoping to minimize any potential conflict arising from the request, is a weak approach, because you put yourself in the position of asking a "favour" that may well be denied. Another bad approach is to be aggressive and try to force someone into giving you what you want. While this can be successful in the short term, it can damage long-term relationships. This will clearly be a problem if you are dealing with your manager.

Favours have no place in the work environment

Be Assertive

Ask for what you want in a fair, reasonable, and positive manner, making your request clearly and openly, explaining rationally why you want it, without trying to use emotional leverage. Keep your request short, direct, and unambiguous. Do not attack or blame the other person for the problem. This is the most effective way to defend your right to a well-balanced life, and to express and get what you want in a manner that is non-manipulative and adult.

How to Get What You Want

HIGH IMPACT	NEGATIVE IMPACT
• Taking an active role	• Adopting a passive role
• Communicating in an adult way	• Taking an inferior position
• Asserting your rights	• Asking for a favour
• Requesting rationally	• Demanding aggressively

Win Support for Your Goals

We have already seen that people in positions of power can have a negative impact on your projects and on your position. With a little effort, some of them could become strong supporters rather than a source of stress.

Manage Your Stakeholders

If you are to progress in your career, it is important to identify potential allies – people who have sufficient influence to make a difference to what you are doing. As you become more successful in your career, the work you do, the actions you take, and the projects you run will affect more and more people. It is vital for your success that these "stakeholders" – especially those with the most power over you – are solidly behind what you are doing. Stakeholder management can ensure that your projects will succeed where others fail, and will enable you to manage the intense politics that are so much a part of the stress of major projects. People who are top achievers in their jobs will usually use the technique of stakeholder management to gain the support they need.

Identify the Stakeholders

Think about who your stakeholders are – all the people who are affected by your work, who have influence or power over it, or who have an interest in its successful (or unsuccessful) conclusion.

At Work	Outside Work
Your manager	The government
Senior executives	Trade associations
Alliance partners	Interest groups
Shareholders	Lenders
Your co-workers	The public
Your team	Prospective customers
Customers	The community
Suppliers	Your family

Analyze Their Interests

Once you have your list of stakeholders, the next step is to work out their power, influence, and interest, so that you can focus your attention and efforts. A good way to do this is to plot the various stakeholders on a Power/Interest Grid. Your manager is likely to have high power and influence over your particular project, as well as a high level of interest. Family members may have high interest, but are unlikely to have much power. People in the high power/high interest quadrant are the ones you must fully engage, and make the greatest efforts to satisfy. Think about how best to communicate with each person, and win his support. Keep people in other quadrants informed, and draw on their support and assistance where you can.

Win the Support of Your Stakeholders

Canvassing the support of the principal stakeholders does much more than simply ensure that they do not hamper your progress and cause you stress.

- The experience, opinions and advice of your principal stakeholders may improve your project and make it more successful.
- Their support can help you to win the resources you need for your project, greatly improving its chances of success.
- Feedback from stakeholders will help you to anticipate people's reactions to your project and enable you to build into your plan the actions and elements that will win support for the project.

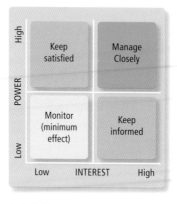

Stakeholder Power/Interest Grid
Focus most of your efforts on the High Power/High Interest stakeholders, but keep others appropriately informed.

"Unreasonable" Demands

Demands that seem unreasonable can be a huge source of stress, although they will often arise through misunderstanding. A simple process of evaluating the demand can go a long way towards reducing the stress.

Avoid Unintentional Pressure

Innocent situations can often reinforce one another to create stressful and unfeasible demands on you. Several customers may be clamouring for the completion of large jobs when you have the resources to service only a few of them. Within your organization, requirements can be misunderstood when they are transmitted from person to person, the importance of deadlines can be overstated, and requests can be made in ignorance of key information.

Consider Your Response

We tend to react emotionally to such demands, feeling that they are being made by a "bad person". In reality, most people are fair and rational, and often the demands are objectively

> **A demand is unreasonable only if there is no good reason for it**

reasonable. In the rare instances when the other person does have a "hidden agenda" and actually wants you to feel or be disadvantaged, you will need to know what course of action is open to you if you refuse to meet the unreasonable demand. You will also need to have an idea of the future value of the relationship, as a sacrifice now may bring benefits later.

Explore the Reasons

People may make seemingly unreasonable demands for a range of good reasons. Perhaps the person making the demand is aware of a consideration that is of great concern to the organization. Always try to find the underlying reason for a demand before dismissing it.

Assess the Demand

When you are faced with an "unreasonable" demand, rather than feeling overwhelmed or responding with anger, make sure of your facts and reach a balanced conclusion in which you can have confidence.

→ Run through the process below, checking at each stage to see whether the demand is, in fact, reasonable.

→ In the case of each demand being made of you, make sure that your response is appropriate.

Make a Good Case

Check your information and assumptions	Make sure you fully understand what you are being asked to do, confirm delivery times, and check whether there is any flexibility in the deadline that you have been given. You may find that the demand isn't as impossible to action as you first thought.
Look at the situation from the other person's perspective	Perhaps he is unaware that you are working at full capacity or that a key member of your team has been seconded to another project. Explain the situation and try to negotiate an appropriate solution.
Explore your alternatives and the cost of each	A little lateral thinking may help you to find a solution that will suit everyone. Evaluate the impact of any possible solution.
Explain your perception assertively	Arrange a meeting and explain the situation to the other person as you see it, in an assertive manner, making your case clearly and without any hint of aggression or frustration. If you behave in a reasonable manner throughout, the other person will probably mirror your good behaviour.
Agree on the best way forward, and manage the consequences	If you really can't agree on a fair way to proceed, one or other of you will have to concede gracefully.

Summary: Being Pro-Active

In your working life, you are subject to various forms of external control. This lack of personal control can be a source of considerable stress. When you find that the demands and influence of others are having a negative effect, the best strategy is usually to take the initiative and talk to those concerned in order to remedy the situation.

Keeping Control of the Situation

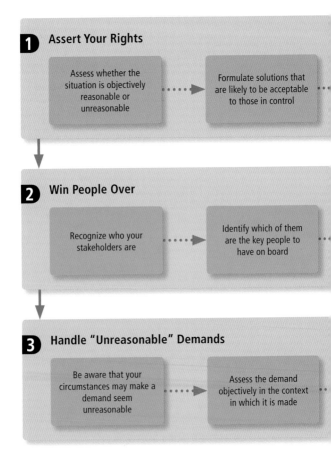

1 Assert Your Rights

Assess whether the situation is objectively reasonable or unreasonable

Formulate solutions that are likely to be acceptable to those in control

2 Win People Over

Recognize who your stakeholders are

Identify which of them are the key people to have on board

3 Handle "Unreasonable" Demands

Be aware that your circumstances may make a demand seem unreasonable

Assess the demand objectively in the context in which it is made

Discuss the problem in a formal context, putting forward your solution calmly and coherently ●●●●● ➤ Reach a solution that will reduce the levels of stress you are experiencing

Approach them early on. Understand their views and take their input into account ●●●●● ➤ Keep all stakeholders informed throughout the project

Explore alternative solutions and evaluate their cost ●●●●● ➤ If you refuse to meet the demand, inform your stakeholders and explain your reasons clearly

Work with Teams

Unhealthy or unproductive relationships with your co-workers can cause great stress, as can working within a dysfunctional team. There are ways to resolve some of the issues that can make teamwork so frustrating.

Consider Team Design and Support

Many of us spend a large part of our time working with the same group of people. When we like these people and enjoy working as part of the team, our work can be very satisfying and we can achieve a great deal. However, if we find our co-workers difficult to deal with and if our teamwork is plagued with conflict, work can become stressful and unpleasant. Problems with working relationships can be a symptom of poor team design or of weak team support and will need to be investigated.

Provide Skills and Resources

A team needs the skills necessary to achieve its goals, as well as access to such resources as information, funding, time, coaching, and support. While we all need to improvise occasionally, it can be intensely frustrating and stressful to be set challenging goals and not have the means to achieve them.

Work Together When individual team members support each other success is almost guaranteed.

Check Team Size

Up to a point, the bigger a team is, the more likely it is to achieve its goals, but size has its disadvantages, too. If your team is large, there are questions you should be asking:

→ Are you having to spend too much time co-ordinating your activities with other team members in order to produce a coherent team product?
→ Are you and your co-workers fully occupied on the team task?
→ Are less-committed team members shirking some of their responsibilities and getting a free ride on the back of other people's efforts?

All of these issues can lead to frustration and stress. If, as a manager, you're having these problems with your team, then you may need to split the team into smaller sub-teams and move some of your best people into supervisory roles.

Reward Appropriately

In a well-designed team, the reward systems are correctly aligned. It is unlikely that a team will function well if bonuses are given to people who succeed at the expense of other team members. If good team behaviour is important to an organization's success, then rewards must reflect this. If your organization is motivating people to behave badly, make sure that you raise this as an issue.

Badly aligned reward systems can undermine team spirit

TIP Some jobs need star performers, and they need to be rewarded appropriately. If possible, do this in a way that doesn't promote jealousy.

Brief the Team

Once the team has been properly designed and brought together, team members need to be briefed clearly so that they know its

Work Together Good teamwork can give you an advantage over apparently stronger opponents and will help you achieve your goals.

purpose, are aware of what they can and can't do, and understand what has to be delivered. This briefing needs to be done carefully if your team is to realize its full potential. Knowing its objectives, the team needs to know what its boundaries are – what it can do and what it cannot do. For example, it needs to know:

- If it can bring more people on to the team
- How far it can change standard working methods
- What power it has to change things outside the team.

A team that does not know its boundaries risks, at one extreme, failing to achieve its potential and, at the other extreme, causing political problems and turf wars. If you don't know what the objectives and boundaries are, make sure you ask. If you're a team leader and you haven't explained these things, make sure you do.

TIP Good coaching can reduce workplace stress by providing problem-solving, team-building, and improved work management skills.

Get Coaching

With good team design and clear briefing, it should be possible to make a good start, but make sure you get coaching, and give it where appropriate. Coaching is one of the most useful and effective management tools and can be used to turn a situation around completely, so that people whose performance was compromised by the levels of stress they were experiencing can become enthusiastic members of the team. Coaching can be motivational, helping people to commit to objectives. It can be educational, helping people to understand how to achieve goals, or helping them to develop essential skills. Coaching can also focus on the team itself, helping individuals to work together effectively.

> **A team needs to know both its objectives and its limits**

think SMART

Teamwork is about communication. If you're the team leader, make sure you give regular feedback. If you're a team member and are not getting feedback from your team leader, make sure you ask for it.

Team members need good feedback on their results. Where problems arise, they need to know about these so that they can correct related behaviour. They also need to be told when results are good; this gives them job satisfaction, increases their self-confidence, and improves the team spirit.

Improve Your Interpersonal Skills

When you have problems working with other people, it is possible that you are contributing to these and to the stress they cause. There may also be team members whose behaviour needs to be negotiated or regulated.

Check Your Expectations

If your team seems to be reasonably well designed and supported, and you are serious about reducing the stress of the team members, you owe it to yourself to consider whether you are part of any problem. If you fail to do this, you risk being severely embarrassed when you raise the matter with other team members. Begin by looking at what you expect from people, and check whether these expectations are fair and reasonable. Try to see things from an objective standpoint. Look at your own attitudes and the way that you relate to people. These can be major contributors to stress, unhappiness, and career failure.

TECHNIQUES *to* practise

The difference between good and bad team behaviour often depends on the situation.
Whenever you have to deal with clients, other companies or outside stakeholders, get into the habit of checking your own behaviour, and that of other people in your team:

- Ask yourself if the way that you or the other people in your team are behaving contributes to or harms the team's delivery.

- Assess the effects of the behaviour on the cohesion or effectiveness of the team. If performance is compromised take steps to change the behaviour in question.
- If the behaviour of individuals in the team is harming the interests of others, speak to them about the negative impact of their actions.
- Take steps to end behaviour that undermines your position as team leader. But try to use negotiation, not manipulation.

Set Team Rules

Teams often establish informal "norms" that govern the way they work together, but occasionally people may lack the sensitivity or social skills to conform to this code of conduct. They may behave in a way that damages the team's delivery to its client, undermines the cohesiveness of the team, or makes other team members unhappy. If assertiveness and negotiation have failed to build good working relationships, more formal rules may be needed.

→ The team should negotiate these "team rules" democratically.
→ Rules should address the problem behaviour.
→ Rules should be formally written down and agreed.
→ If an individual consistently violates these rules, it may be necessary to ask him to leave the team.

Negotiate Change

Occasionally, you will come across team situations where what you want directly conflicts with someone else's interests. Negotiation skills can help you to explore the situation and find a fair solution that is acceptable to both parties. Being aggressive or using tricks and manipulation during negotiations within a team may produce a good result in the short term, but at the cost of severely undermining trust and damaging subsequent teamwork. Remember that the person you are negotiating with is probably someone with whom you will work in future. The best approach is usually to be honest and open during the negotiations, adopting a win-win approach that leaves both parties feeling good about the situation when the negotiation has been concluded. This will help to maintain a positive working relationship afterwards.

> **To handle yourself, use your head; to handle others, use your heart.**
>
> Donald Laird

Reduce
Personal
Stress

4

As well as taking steps to improve your working conditions and your relationships with colleagues, there are many other ways in which you can reduce stress through your approach to stressful events. This chapter will show you how to:

- Prepare for important events and manage performance stress
- Recover from setbacks and learn to build up your self-confidence
- Counter negative thinking effectively
- Analyze your emotions
- Evaluate and manage moods and anxieties

Reduce Performance Stress

We've all had that "sick" feeling before an important presentation. While excessive pressure can undermine your ability to perform well, there are techniques to help you to enjoy, rather than dread, these situations.

Check Your Response

The "inverted-U" relationship between pressure and performance helps to explain why you can "go to pieces" under pressure. The sweaty palms, raised heart rate, and sense of agitation that you feel when you have to perform are the unpleasant side effects of the fight-or-flight response produced by intense pressure. Anxieties and negative thinking crowd your mind, your concentration suffers, your focus narrows, and you find it difficult to think clearly and perform well. So what can you do about overcoming this?

Adjust Your Mindset If you think you're going to enjoy giving a presentation, you will give a good one, and your enthusiasm will be shared by your audience.

TECHNIQUES *to* practise

Part of the stress that you feel comes from uncertainty about what is about to happen. By thinking through the event, you can understand and manage the doubts and uncertainties that may disrupt it.

There are some practical things that you can do before any performance, however small, or however much you are in control of it, to ensure that things go without a hitch.

- Do some research on the situation or environment you will be performing in – if possible, visit it beforehand to familiarize yourself.

- Find out some facts such as the size of your audience, what people will be expecting from your performance, and whether they will be well-disposed towards you.

- Find out if the format will require you to prepare for audience questions.

- Ask what technology will support your performance (lights, sound, projectors, etc.), and what preparations have been made in the event that the technology fails.

Turn It Around

It is worth remembering that stress, managed well, can actually give you a competitive edge. The goal is to find the level of pressure that corresponds to your area of peak performance and enter the "state of flow", in which you are completely involved in an activity for its own sake and where you are using your skills to their limit. Many of the important techniques that help you to manage the performance stress that can disrupt this state of flow come from sport psychology – these are the mental techniques that help top athletes to deliver exceptional performances.

> **Stress is an ignorant state. It believes that everything is an emergency.**
>
> Natalie Goldberg

think
SMART

If you feel happy with your presentation you will feel confident about making it. If you've never made a presentation before, ask a friend to help you to prepare for it using a video camera.

Stand in front of your friend and make your presentation. When you have finished, play back the video together and make a note of things you could improve. Your friend will be able to give you an audience perspective. Amend your presentation and make it again, repeating the process until you are happy with it. This will help you to feel confident on the day of the presentation.

Rehearse Your Performance

Rehearsing for a stressful event, such as an interview or a speech, will polish your performance and build confidence. Practice also allows you to spot any potential problems while you have the opportunity and the time to eliminate them. The more you repeat what you are going to say and do, the smoother and more polished you will become and the better you will perform under pressure.

Be Prepared

For big events, it can be worth preparing a performance plan that helps you to deal with any problems or distractions that may occur and to perform in a positive and focused frame of mind. A plan such as this will give you the confidence that comes from knowing that you are as well prepared for an event as is practically possible. Make a list all of the steps that you need to take, from getting prepared for the performance, through packing, travelling, and setting up, to delivery and conclusion. Work through all of the things that could realistically go wrong and eliminate them by careful preparation.

Rehearse Thoroughly

A good rehearsal makes for a good performance and there are several things you can do to ensure that everything goes smoothly and according to plan.

Plan Your Speech
Rehearse until you're completely fluent and comfortable with what you want to say. If you can, do this in the place where you're going to perform. With enough rehearsal you'll be eloquent under pressure.

Prompt Yourself
Write down your key points on postcards that you can hold and refer to if you lose your place during your presentation. People often won't even notice if you're holding something as small as a prompt card.

Research the Venue
If you're going to show a video as part of your presentation, check that there's a functioning remote-controlled video player and monitor at your venue, and have back-ups in place in case they don't work.

Reduce the Event's Importance

The more important an event is to you, the more stressful it is likely to be. This is particularly true when you are operating at a high level, when many people (especially family or important people) are watching, or when there is the prospect of a large financial reward, promotion, or personal advancement if you perform well. If stress is a problem under these circumstances, take every opportunity to reduce its importance in your eyes. Compare it with bigger events you might know of, or might have attended. Remind yourself that there may be other opportunities for reward later, and this won't be the only chance you have. Focus on the correct performance of your tasks, and the importance of the event will fade into the background.

Get to Know the Venue

If the thought of making a presentation is making you feel very nervous, it is a good idea to reduce the number of unknown factors to a minimum. If it's at all possible, visit the venue where you will be making the presentation so that you can establish where the podium and microphone will be and where you can set up your audio-visual aids. If you are speaking after a number of other speakers, ascertain from where you will be making your entrance. Stand where you will stand during your presentation and visualize a room full of people listening to everything you say.

TIP **If you make a mistake, don't criticize yourself. It is now in the past, and there is nothing you can do about it.**

5minute FIX

If you need to relax before a big event take a few minutes by yourself.

- Sit comfortably with your eyes closed.

- Take slow, deep breaths, inhaling for five seconds, then exhaling for five seconds.

- After 20 breaths, open your eyes and readjust to your surroundings.

Case study: Preparing for Success

Maria was feeling very nervous. She'd just accepted an invitation to speak at a prestigious industry event, and now she was starting to panic about what she'd say.

Realizing that this would be a stressful event, and one that could go badly wrong if she was over-stressed, she planned and prepared carefully. Well before the event, she wrote her speech and polished it so that it was as good as it could be. She took plenty of time preparing her PowerPoint presentation and tweaking it so that it worked smoothly and well. She found out about the venue and the people attending. She prepared for possible eventualities and for difficult questions, and she rehearsed thoroughly. This improved her fluency, and made her feel confident that she'd find her words easily under pressure. After all of this, despite a small power surge while she was making her presentation, she gave the very best speech at the conference, in front of some of the most important decision makers in her industry.

- *Maria's preparation gave her confidence that what she had to say was worth hearing, and meant that she wouldn't have any last-minute self-doubt.*
- *Because she was feeling so confident Maria was able to stay calm even when a few minor things did go wrong.*

Review Your Performance

If you have prepared well, the event will go well, although there will always be things that you feel could have gone better. After the event, make a point of reviewing how things went, how well your preparation served you, how you handled any problems, and what could have been done better. Take confidence from the things that went well and give yourself credit for them. Learn from the things that didn't go as well as you had hoped, and update your performance plan to reflect this. Don't use this review as an opportunity to castigate yourself for everything that you think has gone wrong. In any event, it is unlikely that your audience even noticed the things that didn't go according to plan. And, next time, you'll be even better!

Relax Mentally

Mental relaxation techniques form an important part of your stress "armoury". Used in conjunction with techniques like deep breathing, they are a powerful method of calming your reaction to stressful situations.

Use Imagery to Relax

Imagery is a potent method of stress reduction, especially when combined with physical relaxation methods such as deep breathing. The principle behind imagery is that you can use your imagination to recreate, and enjoy, a relaxing situation. The more intensely you imagine the situation, the more relaxing the experience will be. You can use imagery to prepare for a big event, rehearsing mentally and practising in advance for anything unusual that might occur. Imagery also allows you to pre-experience achievement of your goals to boost your self-confidence. This is a technique that is used by successful athletes.

TECHNIQUES *to* practise

One common use of imagery in relaxation is to imagine a scene or event that you remember as safe, peaceful, and happy. When you are under pressure, sit down in a quiet place, and recall your happy memory.

- Bring all your senses into the image with, for example, sounds of running water and birds, the smell of cut grass, the warmth of the sun.
- Use this happy, beautiful place as a retreat from stress and pressure.
- Imagine all of your stress, distractions, and ordinary, everyday concerns flowing out of your body.

> **Everyone has to find his peace from within . . . and peace, to be real, must be unaffected by outside circumstances.**
>
> Mahatma Gandhi

Meditate Stress Away

By relaxing your body and focusing your thoughts on one thing for a sustained period, your mind is occupied and diverted from the problems that are causing you stress. This gives your body time to relax and recuperate, and to clear away any stress hormones. Begin by sitting quietly and comfortably. Relax your muscles, starting with your feet and working up your body, then use one of the following methods of focusing your concentration:

Learn to Meditate If you find it difficult to get yourself started on meditation, join a meditation class to learn the basic techniques and then use them in your daily life.

- **Focus on your breathing** – With your eyes closed, breathe in deeply and then let your breath out. Do this for ten or 20 minutes.
- **Focus on an object** – Focus your entire attention on an object - its shape, colour differences, texture, temperature, and movement.
- **Focus on a mental image** – This can be a very refreshing way to meditate. Here, you create a mental image of a pleasant and relaxing place.

It is important to keep your attention focused. If external thoughts or distractions wander into your mind, let them drift out until you can focus your mind again.

Use Self-Hypnosis

Hypnosis has a dubious image, but it is a useful tool for achieving deep relaxation. Like meditation, self-hypnosis helps you to relax your body, allows stress hormones to subside, and distracts your mind from unpleasant thoughts. The relaxation achieved with self-hypnosis can be intense. Together with meditation and imagery, self-hypnosis can be used as part of a comprehensive daily stress management routine.

Use Affirmations

Unlike meditation, self-hypnosis can be combined with affirmations (positive statements) to manage stress and build self-confidence. If you want to use positive affirmations, prepare them before you start the session, as you will not want to think about them once you have achieved a state of deep relaxation.

TECHNIQUES *to* practise

The two principal elements of self-hypnosis are relaxation and suggestion. Once you have relaxed your body you can utilize the power of suggestion to deepen your state of relaxation, introducing affirmations to your suggestion, if you believe that this will be beneficial.

• Begin by finding somewhere comfortable and quiet, and sitting down. Close your eyes, and imagine waves of relaxation running through your body from your scalp downwards, washing out any stress you feel.

• Use suggestion to deepen the state of relaxation. This can be as simple as saying, "I am feeling relaxed and comfortable" to yourself, or you might use the traditional approach of telling yourself that you are tired and sleepy.

• Once you feel completely relaxed, mix in the affirmations you have prepared with the relaxation suggestions.

Use Bio-Feedback

Imagery and other relaxation techniques can be shown to work by using biofeedback devices.

→ These are electronic sensors that measure indicators of your stress levels, such as the electrical conductance of your skin, and feed them back as a dial reading or an audible signal.

→ This enables you to observe for yourself the real effect of these relaxation techniques.

→ By imagining pleasant and unpleasant scenes, for example, you can actually see or hear the levels of stress in your body decreasing or increasing.

Let Sound Relax You

Imagery, meditation, and self-hypnosis are all active mental techniques that require concentration. An alternative, and equally valid, approach is to listen to calming music, or to pre-recorded relaxation MP3s or hypnosis CDs. It requires no effort to listen to these, and this may be very welcome at the end of a long, hard day's work. If you commute by public transport, try listening to them on a personal stereo as you travel home from work. Soothing music and natural sounds can also be used to accompany the more active relaxation methods discussed here. You can buy relaxing music in many places, including several specialist websites, but an alternative approach is to record tapes for yourself and develop routines tailored to your needs.

There's a relaxation technique to suit everyone

TIP Don't use sound as a source of relaxation when you're driving – you need to stay alert!

Relax Your Body

Physical relaxation techniques can help you to reduce muscle tension and manage the effects on your body of the fight-or-flight response. This can be particularly important if you need to think clearly and perform.

Breathe Deeply

Deep breathing is a simple, but very effective, method of relaxation, and it is a core component of everything from the "take ten deep breaths" approach to calming someone down, right through to yoga relaxation and Zen meditation. It works well in conjunction with other relaxation techniques such as progressive muscular relaxation (see opposite), relaxation imagery, and meditation to reduce stress. To use the technique, simply take a number of deep breaths and relax your body further with each breath. That's all there is to it, but it works!

Learn Mental and Physical Control Techniques

By practising any of the relaxation techniques in this chapter, you will gain some control over your mental and physical stress responses. The use of bio-feedback technology will help you in this, but even just taking your pulse will help you to gauge how stressed you are, and you can learn to deliberately raise and lower your heartbeat by, for example, imagining stressful and restful situations alternately. These techniques will make you more aware of when stress is having an effect on you, and enable you to take conscious steps to calm yourself down.

5 minute FIX

If you need to release stress-induced neck tension quickly, repeat this simple exercise 5–10 times.

- Sit in a comfortable position and close your eyes.
- Bring your shoulders up to your ears.
- Hold the position for five seconds.
- Relax slowly into your starting position.

Discover Progressive Muscular Relaxation

In a series of experiments into various forms of meditation in the 1960s, Dr Herbert Benson of Harvard University established that this technique really does help to reduce stress and control the fight-or-flight response.

The technique is essentially the same as meditation, but it focuses on the physical effects. These physical effects include deep relaxation, slowed heartbeat and breathing, reduced oxygen consumption, and increased skin resistance.

→ Sit quietly and comfortably, and close your eyes.
→ Start by relaxing the muscles of your feet and then work your way up your body, relaxing the muscles in sequence.
→ Focus your attention on your breathing.
→ Breathe in deeply and then let your breath out.
→ Count your breaths, and say the number of each breath as you let it out.
→ Continue doing this for between ten and 20 minutes.

RELAXATION
RESPONSE

Reduce stress

Sit quietly

Think of a relaxing image

Relax muscles

Breathe deeply

Focus on breathing

Use Imagery An even more potent approach is to follow these steps, but to use relaxation imagery instead of counting breaths.

TIP Use these relaxation techniques whenever you need to perform well under pressure.

Think Rationally

While taking action to change the situation is one way of managing and reducing stress, perception-oriented techniques can reduce stress by changing the way you see, and therefore feel about, a situation.

Don't Put Yourself Down

In many cases, it is not the situation that causes stress, but the way we react to it and what we say to ourselves about it. Often we can be too harsh on ourselves. Negative thinking of this kind can cause intense stress and unhappiness, and can damage your performance by undermining your self-confidence and distracting you when you need to focus on what you're doing. You are thinking negatively when you fear the future, put yourself down, criticize yourself for errors, doubt your abilities, or expect failure.

You can't manage your thoughts until you are aware of them

Become Aware

The first step in learning how to deal with negative thoughts is to recognize that you are having them. Unfortunately, these thoughts tend to flit in and out of our consciousness almost unnoticed, and because of this they certainly go unchallenged. These negative thoughts can be completely incorrect, but this doesn't diminish their harmful effect. Thought awareness can be achieved by observing and recording your stream of consciousness as you think about a stressful situation. Don't suppress any thoughts; just let them run their course while you watch them unfold and jot them down as they happen.

TIP If you find it hard to be objective, look at your list of negative thoughts and imagine how someone else would challenge them.

think
SMART

You may find that simply writing down in your stress diary all of your negative thoughts and the things that you are worried about will give you a better perspective on your problems.

Try to log all of your negative thoughts and anxieties in your stress diary as they occur, then tackle the most common and damaging ones – these are the things that are interfering with your enjoyment of life. By learning to deal effectively with the problem areas of your life you will soon start finding solutions to difficulties as they arise and will be able to take advantage of opportunities for improving your quality of life.

Challenge Negative Thoughts

Your stress diary may reveal that you often have feelings of inadequacy, are worried that your performance in your job will not be good enough, or are anxious about other people's reactions to your work. Always ask yourself whether a negative thought is reasonable: does it stand up to scrutiny? Challenge your negative thoughts.

- **Feelings of inadequacy** – Do you have the experience and resources you need to do your job? Have you planned, prepared, and rehearsed appropriately? If you have done all of these, perhaps you are setting yourself unattainably high standards for doing the job.
- **Worries about performance** – Are you properly trained? Have you prepared properly? Do you have enough time? If not, then you need to take action quickly. If the answer is yes, then you are well positioned to give the best performance that you can.
- **Anxiety about other people's reactions** – If you have put in good preparation, and you do the best you can, then that is all that you need to know. If you perform as well as you can, fair people are likely to respond well.

Heed the Warning

By challenging negative thoughts rationally, you should be able to determine accurately whether the thoughts are wrong or whether they reflect a realistic appraisal of the situation. If there is some substance to your concerns, work to take appropriate action. In these cases, negative thinking has been an early warning system showing where you need to direct your attention.

Produce Positive Thoughts

Where you have used rational thinking to identify incorrect negative thinking, you'll be able to turn these around by preparing rational positive thoughts and affirmations to counter your negative thoughts. The danger with negative thoughts is that they can begin to dictate to you what the reality is, blocking you from any possibility of making an objective assessment of a situation. Rational thinking will help you to produce realistic positive thoughts. Using realistic positive affirmations can help you to build your self-confidence and reverse the damaging effects of negative thinking.

We usually fail because we fear failure

Think Positive

HIGH IMPACT

- Writing down your negative thoughts when they occur
- Challenging your negative thoughts objectively
- Using affirmations to counter "unfair" thoughts
- Exploring opportunities that arise from positive thinking

NEGATIVE IMPACT

- Letting your negative thoughts go unchecked
- Accepting your negative thinking as reality
- Worrying about situations without taking action
- Thinking positively without thinking rationally

Counteract your negative thoughts with positive statements that will increase your confidence.
You can practise counteracting negative thinking with some positive affirmations:

- Feelings of inadequacy: "I am well trained for this. I have the experience, the resources, and the knowledge I need. I can do a superb job."
- Worries about performance: "I have researched and planned well for this, and I thoroughly understand the problem.

I have the time, resources, and help I need. I am ready to do an excellent job."

- Worry about other people's reaction: "I am well prepared and am doing the best I can. Fair people will respect this. I will rise above any unfair criticism in a mature and professional way."
- Write these affirmations down, then repeat them to yourself a few times whenever you are feeling undermined and your confidence could do with a boost.

Take the Opportunities

Pushing positive thinking one step further, it can also be useful to look at the situation and see whether it offers any useful opportunities. In the examples above, if you successfully overcome the situations causing the negative thinking, you will acquire new skills and be seen as someone who can handle difficult challenges. This, in turn, may open up new career possibilities and will give you the confidence to take advantage of any new opportunities that present themselves. Initially, each time a new challenge presents itself you may find that you need to repeat your positive affirmations, However, after having dealt successfully with several difficult situations you may find that you no longer need them.

TIP **Affirmations will be strongest if they are specific and expressed in the present tense.**

Analyze Your Emotions

Emotional analysis will help you to understand your emotions and what they are telling you. You can decide whether they are correct or not, and either change your interpretation of the situation or take action.

Use Your Emotions

Excessive emotions such as intense anger have tremendous power to damage the complex social relationships on which we rely. They can also lead to rash and unwise actions. However, this is only part of the story. Like the fight-or-flight reflex, negative emotions give us the benefit of a speedy, and sometimes effective, response to simple situations, at the cost of a sophisticated and reliable analysis of more complex ones. Even if instant action is not required, our emotions can alert us to something to which we need to pay attention. We can then utilize more sophisticated analysis techniques to understand the situation in detail.

Read the Signals What someone says may not be what she means. Read the emotions behind the words.

Check Your Fundamental Assumptions

There are six main automatic assumptions that can lie beneath negative emotions. The specific emotions we experience in a difficult situation depend on which of these assumptions or factors apply. These assumptions are:

→ The situation is relevant to our goals.
→ The situation threatens our goals.
→ The situation will turn out badly.
→ Something important to us is being threatened.
→ We are responsible, or someone else is to blame.
→ We have some power to affect the situation, or we have no power at all.

Hear the Warnings

Emotions can be an important early warning system. We experience different negative emotions for different reasons, and we experience the emotion because we are making specific subconscious assumptions about the situation. For example, we feel anger because we are subconsciously assuming that someone or something is frustrating goals that are important to us. Emotional analysis can help us to get to the root of why we are experiencing negative emotions and look closely at whether the information they are communicating to us is right or wrong. If the assumptions we are making about a situation turn out to be correct, we can learn from the early warning signals and do whatever we can to change the situation. If our assumptions are incorrect, we can change the way we see the situation.

> **Emotions can be a useful early warning signal of a problem**

TECHNIQUES
to practise

When you experience a negative emotion, follow the steps below to carry out an emotional analysis. If you practise this type of analysis regularly, it will soon start to come naturally to you.

- Use relaxation techniques to calm yourself down so that you can think clearly about why you are upset.
- Identify your assumptions. Using the list of fundamental assumptions and the list of emotions and assumptions opposite as a checklist, work through them and identify the assumptions that you are currently making.
- Challenge each of the assumptions rationally to see whether it is correct or not.

Don't be harsh with yourself – be fair. If it helps, imagine as you make each challenge that you are your best friend.

- Take appropriate action. When your assumptions are incorrect, the negative emotion should change or disappear as soon as you acknowledge this. If there is some element of truth to an assumption, recognize this and consider how to manage the situation. It may be possible to derive energy from the emotion, and motivation to achieve what you need to achieve. Remember that controlled, well-founded anger can actually be hugely motivating and enormously powerful.

Analyze Your Anger

As an example, suppose that you have identified that you are angry and you recognize the assumptions listed against "anger" in the table opposite. The next step is to challenge these assumptions by asking rational questions such as: "What goals are being challenged? Are they important? Are they really being frustrated? How severe is the damage? Am I attributing blame fairly?" Likewise, if you have identified that you feel shame, ask yourself if the ideal you have created is realistic. Ask similar questions about any assumptions that you are making.

Check Your Assumptions

Psychologist Richard S. Lazarus (and others) proposed a theory stating that we experience different emotions for different reasons, some of which we understand consciously, but some of which we process subconsciously.

→ The emotions we experience depend on our assumptions.

→ Where our assumptions are correct, our emotions alert us to situations to which we need to pay some attention.

→ Where they are incorrect, we can act impulsively and foolishly.

Are Your Assumptions Correct?

Emotion	Assumption
Anger The feeling that a demeaning offence has been committed against us and ours	Important goals have been frustrated; our self-esteem, or people, objects, or ideas that we value are damaged; others are to blame.
Anxiety The feeling of facing an uncertain, existential threat	Our survival or what we hold to be important is under threat; we are uncertain about whether the threatened situation will occur and we are unsure about its severity; no one is to blame.
Fright The feeling of facing an immediate, concrete, and overwhelming danger	There is a threat to our survival or to what we hold to be important; no one is to blame.
Guilt The feeling of having transgressed a moral imperative	We have failed to live up to an important moral standard; we place the blame for this on ourselves.
Shame The feeling of having failed to live up to an ego ideal	We have failed to live up to an ideal of ourselves; we blame this on ourselves.
Sadness The feeling of having experienced an irrevocable loss	Our self-esteem, or people, objects, or ideas that we value have been damaged; no one is really to blame; we are unable to recover the situation.

Manage Unhappy Moods

Sometimes negative thinking is more than a passing emotion and becomes a more pervasive mood. Cognitive restructuring will help you to challenge your negative moods and change the thinking that lies behind them.

Turn Your Mood Around

Negative moods are not only unpleasant – they reduce the quality of your performance and undermine your working and social relationships. Cognitive restructuring can help you to turn these moods around so that you can approach situations in a more positive frame of mind. The principle behind this technique is that our moods are driven by what we tell ourselves, and that this, in turn, is based on our interpretation of our environment.

Case study: Managing Unhappy Moods

Melinda had been feeling unhappy for weeks. She'd had a big argument with Alicia, one of her best friends at her new job. Having good friends at work was important to her, and she was feeling miserable and insecure. She spoke about this to her partner who suggested that she should analyze why she was feeling as she did.

Identifying her dominant mood as "rejected", her thoughts were, "she doesn't like me any more, and, "she doesn't think I'm good enough to be her friend." As supporting evidence, she cited the aggression and anger she'd faced from Alicia. However, thinking about the opposing evidence, she remembered that Alicia had seemed quite shame-faced after the argument and had seemed to want to talk, but hadn't. She also remembered that she had been having family problems.

• *Taking a balanced view, Melinda realized that Alicia's personal problems had spilled over into her working life and were having an effect on their relationship.*
• *Melinda resolved to be warm and friendly the next day and to talk through any problems. Alicia's friendship with her was soon back on track.*

Cognitive Restructuring

Cognitive restructuring is a useful technique to use when you identify that you are in an unhappy mood. This might be when you are sad, angry, anxious, upset, or in one of many other negative states of mind. It can also be used if you note that you are frequently experiencing bad moods of a particular type or in particular circumstances.

What Triggered Your Mood?	**Example**
When you are aware that you have experienced a negative mood, record the details of the event or situation that has triggered it.	You may have been in a meeting with other members of your team when your manager rejected, out of hand, a suggestion that you made.
What Was Your Mood?	**Example**
Identify the deep feelings that you had. Moods are not thoughts. Moods can usually be expressed in one word, while thoughts are more complex. You may have felt several different moods at the same time. .	For example, "He is trashing my suggestion in front of my co-workers," would be a thought, while the associated moods might be "humiliation", "frustration", "anger", or "insecurity".

Change the Way You Think

Where issues are difficult and important and require a careful, considered examination, cognitive restructuring enables you to examine how rational and valid your interpretations are, and, if appropriate, to test them. Where you find that your interpretations of a situation are incorrect, this will naturally change the way you think about that situation and will change your mood. If you find that you frequently experience a negative mood in response to events, it is worth taking the time to learn the technique of cognitive restructuring.

TIP If unhappy moods persist and you feel that you may be becoming depressed, it is important that you see a doctor for advice.

Write Down Your Automatic Thoughts

Begin the restructuring process by writing down the particular thoughts that spring into your mind when you feel unhappy. For example:

- Everyone will think badly of me
- Maybe my analysis skills aren't good enough
- How rude and arrogant of him!
- This is undermining my future with this organization

Identify the most distressing of these – the "hot thoughts". In this case, the first two thoughts might be regarded as the hot thoughts.

Note Supporting and Contradictory Evidence

Identify the objective evidence that supports these hot thoughts. If you are in a meeting, for example, you might write down that the discussion moved on without any account being taken of your suggestion, and that your boss did identify a flaw in one of the arguments in your paper on the subject.

Next, identify the objective evidence that does not support the hot thoughts. You might write down that the flaw in your argument was minor and didn't alter the conclusions reached, that your analysis was objectively sound, that the suggestion was well founded, and that your clients respect your analysis and opinions.

Deal with Hot Thoughts

HIGH IMPACT

- Understanding your moods
- Taking a serious approach to your unhappy moods
- Understanding what lies behind your moods
- Evaluating supporting and opposing evidence
- Taking positive action

NEGATIVE IMPACT

- Getting stuck in a cycle of negative thinking
- Not seeing hot thoughts as being of importance
- Experiencing without analyzing
- Accepting negative thinking without thought
- Letting bad situations persist

TECHNIQUES *to* practise

The cognitive restructuring technique consists of a seven-step process.

Record your findings at each stage by writing them on a sheet of paper divided into seven columns.

1 Write down details of the situation that triggered the negative thoughts.

2 Identify the moods that you experienced while you were in the situation.

3 Write down the immediate distressing thoughts that you experienced when you felt the negative mood.

4 Identify the evidence that exists to supports these "hot thoughts".

5 Identify the evidence that contradicts the hot thoughts.

6 Identify fair, balanced thoughts about the situation.

7 Observe your mood and think about what you'll do.

Look at Both Sides

It's important to look at the situation objectively. If there are still substantial points of uncertainty, discuss the situation with other people who have a view. The balanced thoughts in the meeting example might now be: "Other people respect my abilities. My analysis was reasonable, but not perfect. There was an error, but the conclusions were valid. People were shocked by the way he handled my suggestion."

A fair analysis is likely to produce a fair solution

Decide What You're Going to Do

Finally, observe your mood now and think about what action you are going to take. Hopefully your mood has improved. You should now have a clearer view of the situation. You may conclude that no action is appropriate. By looking at the situation in a balanced way, it may cease to be important.

Summary: Changing Perception

Stress is what you experience when you feel that you are not in control. Thinking rationally and positively about a situation, being objective about your emotions and what they are telling you, and challenging your negative moods can all help you to reduce stress significantly and allow you to regain some control over your life.

Changing the Way You Think

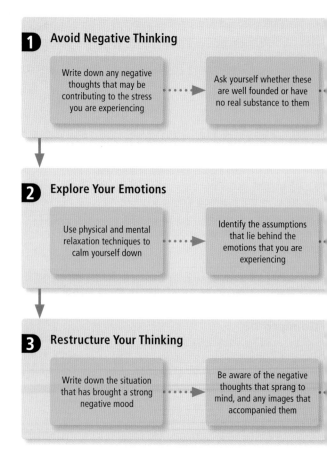

1 Avoid Negative Thinking

Write down any negative thoughts that may be contributing to the stress you are experiencing

Ask yourself whether these are well founded or have no real substance to them

2 Explore Your Emotions

Use physical and mental relaxation techniques to calm yourself down

Identify the assumptions that lie behind the emotions that you are experiencing

3 Restructure Your Thinking

Write down the situation that has brought a strong negative mood

Be aware of the negative thoughts that sprang to mind, and any images that accompanied them

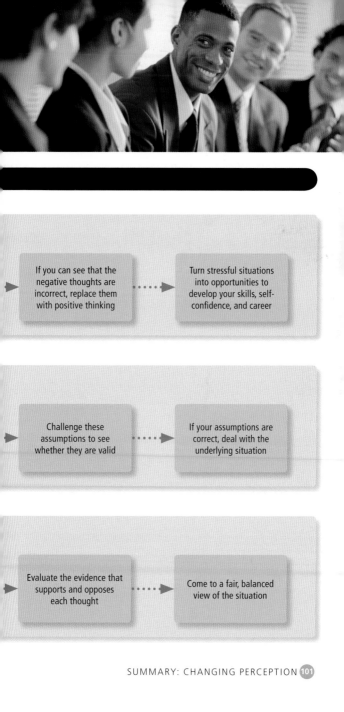

If you can see that the negative thoughts are incorrect, replace them with positive thinking ······▶ Turn stressful situations into opportunities to develop your skills, self-confidence, and career

Challenge these assumptions to see whether they are valid ······▶ If your assumptions are correct, deal with the underlying situation

Evaluate the evidence that supports and opposes each thought ······▶ Come to a fair, balanced view of the situation

Survive Long-Term Stress

5

Now that you have looked at specific techniques that you can use as you work to counter particular sources of stress, this final chapter takes a broader look at reducing the long-term accumulation of stress through the use of support networks and leading a healthy lifestyle. You will also discover ways of avoiding or surviving stress-induced burnout. This chapter will help you to:

- Defend yourself against stress
- Understand what burnout is about and identify the danger signals
- Check your own risk of burnout
- Avoid burnout or cope with it if it happens

Build Defences Against Stress

If stress is an inherent part of your job, you can take steps to defend yourself against its effects. There are support networks that you can call upon, and ways of adjusting your lifestyle to maximize your resilience.

Look for Help

When you are under intense stress, it is very natural to withdraw from the world and concentrate exclusively on solving the problem that is causing the stress. Sometimes this is a useful and appropriate reaction, but often it is not, especially as your projects become larger and more complex. One person working on his own simply cannot achieve tasks that are greater than a certain size. Similarly, many stressful situations cannot be resolved without looking for and getting the help of other people.

Use Support Networks

We all have networks of people who can help us to solve problems. In the context of your work, your professional networks include relationships with a range of people within your organization, including your manager, mentors, colleagues, your team, and the organizational support services. External people who offer support include professional contacts, clients, suppliers, trade associations, professional, state, and independent organizations (some of which may exist solely to help you to solve the problem you face). Outside work, your social networks obviously include your friends, clubs, social organizations, and, importantly, your close and extended family. Don't be afraid to ask for appropriate help where it is available. A request for help shows that you are sufficiently in control of the situation to realize that it's more than you can cope with on your own.

Help will usually arrive when it's sent for

Call for Assistance

People in your social and professional networks can give help and support in a wide variety of ways.

→ **Physical assistance** – This can be financial or direct help, or the provision of useful resources.

→ **Political assistance** – Other people can use their influence and personal networks on your behalf to help with the situation, for example, by persuading other people to move deadlines, change what they are doing, or help directly.

→ **Information** – People may have information that helps in the situation or solves the problem, or they may have personal experience that can help you.

→ **Problem solving** – These people may be able to help you to think through how to solve the problem. They may have solved the problem before or seen it solved elsewhere. Just explaining a problem clearly to someone else can bring it into focus so that the solution is obvious. People in your network may have problem-solving skills that you do not, or may just be sufficiently fresh and unstressed to see good alternatives.

→ **Reassurance** – Friends and colleagues can give emotional support and reassurance when you may be starting to doubt yourself. They can help you to put problems into context or can help you to find solace elsewhere. Others can simply cheer you up when you are feeling down.

Have a Support Circle
Depending on the type of difficulty you are having, you may want to turn to one or more circles in your support network to take some of the pressure off when you are feeling stressed.

Help

Support

SUPPORT CIRCLE

Influence

Solution

Experience

Rest and Relax

When people who are highly committed to their work are faced with a stressful situation, they often respond by working intensely hard to resolve it, cancelling holidays, and cutting back on sleep and recreation. In the short term, the negative effects may be minimal and success can be spectacular, but if this level of work is sustained for a long time there is a risk of burnout. Relaxation – at the end of a working day and at the end of a working week – will help you to calm down and allow your stress to subside.

Take Some Time Out

A Saturday afternoon spent on a hobby will give you enough perspective to refocus on your priorities at work and in life.

Have Some Fun

Doing things that you enjoy in your leisure time compensates you for the stress you experience at work, bringing back some balance into life. If you spend all your working day competing, then a non-competitive sport or hobby is a good way of reducing long-term stress. Slow physical activities, where there is little or no pressure for performance, such as sailing, fishing, or walking, are good for this. Reading, watching television, or socializing with friends can also be restful. By offsetting the unpleasant and stressful events in your life against plenty of good, enjoyable, and relaxing events, you will make your life more tolerable and reduce the risk of burnout.

Case study: Keeping the Balance

Jean was feeling ground down and irritable. His work was so intensive that he found himself cancelling holidays and working long hours to stay on top of his workload. He was always tired, increasingly irritable, and was not enjoying his work. His relationships at work and home were suffering, and life was increasingly gruelling.

Jean knew that this couldn't continue. He booked a two-week holiday at a remote beach club and said that he would be out of contact while there. He had a great time on holiday with his partner and the slow, relaxed pace of the resort ensured that he returned to work recharged and re-energized.

• *Jean had realized in time that he was getting into a vicious circle of overwork and fatigue in which his effectiveness was being diminished by stress.*
• *The pressure of work had been causing him to distance himself from people around him, increasing his stress.*
• *Taking a break gave him renewed energy and vigour so that he was able to re-engage with his team and his work and rebalance his workload.*

TIP **Take regular holidays – they will help you to reduce stress and gain some valuable perspective on your working situation.**

Get Plenty of Sleep

If you are regularly short of sleep, your concentration and effectiveness will suffer and your energy levels decline. This can reduce your control over events and make an already difficult and stressful situation worse. If you have become used to being tired all the time, you will be amazed at how sharp and energetic you will feel once you start sleeping normally. Give yourself at least an hour to wind down before going to bed. Take a warm bath while listening to soothing music, or watch something amusing on TV.

Make sure that your bedroom is restful, calming, well-ventilated, and cool. It should be comfortable and without any distractions or irritations. Avoid using your bedroom as a workplace – this will create an association with the stressful and difficult situations that you need to forget.

Take Exercise

As well as improving your health and reducing the stress caused by unfitness, frequent exercise also relaxes the muscles and helps you to sleep. There are other positive benefits, too.

→ Exercise improves blood flow to the brain, bringing additional sugars and oxygen that may be needed when you are actively engaged in thinking intensely.

→ It speeds the flow of blood through your brain, removing waste products faster and improving brain function.

→ It can cause the release of chemicals called endorphins into your blood stream. These give you a feeling of happiness, and positively affect your overall wellbeing.

→ Physically fit people have less extreme physiological responses when under pressure than those who are unfit, making them better able to handle the long-term effects of stress.

Seek the advice of a trained medical professional before engaging actively in any type of exercise programme.

Watch Your Diet

You need to keep up your energy levels when you're feeling stressed. What you eat is extremely important. Cut down on salt and sugar and eat unrefined carbohydrates such as wholemeal bread and oats. Eat plenty of fresh fruit and vegetables, and cut down on your consumption of caffeine and alcohol. Stress depletes the body of essential B vitamins so make sure to include eggs, poultry, pulses, nuts, and seeds in your diet. It can be worth taking a multivitamin and mineral supplement.

Take Time to Eat

Usually, when we're under a lot of pressure, the first casualty of a normal life is a proper mealtime. We tend to eat on the run, picking up whatever snack we can and eating it at the desk or in the car while en route to the next appointment. It's important to take time to sit down while eating and to eat slowly. If you eat too quickly you won't chew properly and will probably eat too much.

Deal with Burnout

Burnout is a very real threat to people in challenging and stressful jobs. It mainly strikes highly-committed, passionate, hard-working, and successful people, who lose all motivation and interest in their work.

What is Burnout?

According to Ayala Pines and Elliott Aronson, burnout is "a state of physical, emotional and mental exhaustion caused by long-term involvement in emotionally demanding situations." Herbert J. Freudenberger defines it as "A state of fatigue or frustration brought about by devotion to a cause, way of life, or relationship that failed to produce the expected reward."

Understand Burnout

These definitions embrace the two key components of burnout – exhaustion and disillusionment. Together they highlight the irony of burnout. Anyone can become exhausted, but burnout only strikes people who are highly committed to their work. While exhaustion can be overcome with rest, a core part of burnout is a deep sense of disillusionment and a loss of a sense of meaning.

Get Away from It All
Making time to relax and think about the things you value in life can help you to avoid burnout.

Recognize the Symptoms of Burnout

As you get less satisfaction from your work, the downsides of the job become more troublesome. As you get more tired you have less energy to give and it becomes more difficult to stay on top of an increasingly demanding workload.

If your organization fails to support you, you can grow increasingly disenchanted with it and lose faith in what you are doing. You can become cynical and disenchanted. This is full-scale burnout.

Physical Symptoms

These are much as you would expect them to be and can include:

→ Physical fatigue
→ Frequent illness
→ Sleep problems

Emotional Symptoms

These may include:

→ Disillusionment with the job
→ The loss of a sense of meaning
→ Cynicism towards the organization
→ Feelings of frustration, and a lack of power to change events
→ Strong feelings of anger against those you hold responsible
→ Feelings of depression and isolation

> **High achievers, in particular, should watch for burnout**

Behavioural Symptoms

These reflect exhaustion and a loss of satisfaction with work:

→ Increasing detachment from co-workers
→ Increased absenteeism
→ An increased harshness in dealing with your teams
→ A marked reduction in your commitment to your work
→ Increased alcohol consumption

One symptom of an approaching nervous breakdown is the belief that one's work is terribly important.

Bertrand Russell

Find the Right Level

Many of us get our sense of identity and meaning from our work. We may have started our careers with high ideals or high ambitions and may have followed these with passion. We are hard-working, effective, full of initiative, energetic, and selfless. Not surprisingly, with this level of commitment and resilience, we are often spectacularly successful at what we do.

Avoid Over-Commitment

The trouble starts when things become too much for us. It's not just that we are exhausted. Other factors come into play, too. The problems that we are facing start to seem too large, or we lack the resources that we need. Perhaps supportive mentors move on and are replaced by people who do not subscribe to the same ideals as us. Maybe we feel that we are no longer appreciated, or the physical and emotional demands on us are just too great. This can be where burnout begins to set in.

Talk it Over If you are having problems at work, share them with a supportive colleague, who may have dealt with a similar situation before.

Check Yourself for Burnout

Rate each question on a scale of 1–5,
where 1 = Not at all and 5 = Very often.

	Rating
Do you feel run down and drained of physical or emotional energy?	☐
Do you find that you are prone to negative thinking about your job?	☐
Do you find yourself getting easily irritated by small problems, or by your co-workers and team?	☐
Do you feel misunderstood or unappreciated by your co-workers?	☐
Do you feel that you have no one to talk to?	☐
Do you feel that you are achieving less than you should?	☐
Do you feel under an unpleasant level of pressure to succeed?	☐
Do you feel that you are not getting what you want out of your job?	☐
Do you feel that you have more work than you have the ability to do?	☐

Now add up the scores and check them against this list.

10–12	You show no signs of burnout.
13–21	There is little sign that you are at risk of burnout.
22–29	Be careful – you may be at risk of burnout.
30–39	You are at severe risk of burnout – do something about this urgently.
40–45	You are at very severe risk of burnout – do something about this with the greatest urgency.

Take Steps to Avoid Burnout

If you are at risk of burnout and you intend to do something to improve the situation, you need to identify which areas of work are at the root of the problem, and then take practical remedial steps.

Identify the Pressure Points

Identify the most important sources of long-term and day-to-day stress in your life. These are likely to fall into four categories – excessive workload, people problems, personal exhaustion, and disillusionment.

Reduce the Load

If excessive workload is the problem, see if you can cut out any low-yield jobs. Are you managing your time as well as possible? Could you delegate more tasks to other people? Then consider whether you are being too accommodating. Perhaps you should be more assertive in letting people know that you have too much work and can't take on more. Are you using all of the resources available to you, including your support network? Finally, check that you're not being asked to handle a project that no one else wants because the organization simply does not have the capabilities, resources, or skills to bring it to completion.

Limit the Damage

HIGH IMPACT	NEGATIVE IMPACT
• Taking serious action to avoid burnout	• Allowing emergencies to delay action
• Managing the stressful situation assertively	• Hoping that people will notice that you're unhappy
• Cutting back on any unnecessary activities	• Hoping that things will get better without action
• Refocusing on activities that you find satisfying	• Distancing yourself from the people you need
• Getting enough rest	• Never taking any holidays

Strike a Balance

If "politics" seems to be a problem, check that you are allocating enough time to managing your stakeholders and that you are correctly managing your support network. Don't stop communicating. However, you do need to find a balance between being available to the people with whom you live and work, and distancing yourself from people who drain you emotionally. You also need to balance the demands of different groups of people. An obvious conflict is between work and family. You need to find a way of reconciling these, while still leaving time for yourself.

You can only burn out if you were alight in the first place

Protect the Meaning of Your Job

Another major cause of burnout can be disillusionment with your job. Focus on protecting those parts of your job that give you the most meaning and satisfaction. If the job itself is badly designed, or inherent contradictions are causing you stress, analyze it to check it out, and do what you can to improve your situation. If frustration with a lack of career development is the problem, look again at career planning and establish whether you need to move on.

Cope with Burnout

It may be too late to talk about avoiding burnout. Perhaps you have reached a stage where you are disillusioned with your job and are now just going through the motions. Where do you go from here?

Change Careers

If you have lost all interest in the values that led you into your profession in the first place, then a career change may be the only option. However, you may well lose the benefit of the precious experience that you have gained within the profession, and you may be competing equally with younger people who are willing to accept lower salaries. You may also feel a strong sense of failure, whereas burnout will have been only a temporary setback if you can turn the situation around.

Change Jobs

A job change is appropriate if you are disillusioned with your organization rather than your career. You will bring with you many of your skills and much of your experience, and you can rededicate yourself to your original goals in a new environment. Make sure that you understand the causes of your burnout and that history does not repeat itself. Be aware of the stresses of a new job.

think SMART

People can survive stress for quite a long time and then suddenly collapse. To avoid this happening to you, take steps to protect yourself from burnout. Doing nothing is not an option.

Talk to people about how you feel, take a holiday before you're completely exhausted, and think about how you can improve your life by removing some of the more stressful elements and achieving a better balance.

Turn Burnout into Personal Growth

The most positive way to manage burnout is to treat it as a wake-up call, an opportunity to re-evaluate the way you want to live your life and what you want to achieve.

→ **Why did it happen?** – Deal with the sense of failure by taking a hard, dispassionate look at the circumstances leading up to it. Talk the situation through with someone you trust, looking at your workload, your actions, and those of others, and how the situation evolved. No doubt you made some mistakes, but a good deal of the blame probably lies with the situation, your colleagues, or those who set up the situation.

→ **Determine your goals** – Re-evaluate your goals and think about what you want to achieve with your life, giving due weight to relaxation, the quality of life issues, and the social activities that will help to protect you against burnout in the future. Make sure that your goals do not conflict, and that they are not so challenging that they become a source of excessive stress in their own right.

→ **Make a new start** – Assess your current position with respect to these goals using SWOT analysis, and identify where you need to develop new skills or solicit the help of other people. Make an action plan and start to work on it. This may include changing job or career, but you will be doing this as part of an active plan for the future, not as an escape.

Burnout often results in people taking a long hard look at what they are doing with their lives. They re-evaluate their priorities and focus on living a life that is worthwhile to them.

Come Back from Burnout

Assess the damage

Make an action plan

Re-evaluate your goals

Index

Picture Credits

The publisher would like to thank the following for their kind permission to reproduce their photographs: Abbreviations key : (l) = left, (c) = centre, (r) = right, (t) = top, (b) = below, (cl) = centre left, (cr) = centre right.

1: Jerome Tisne/Iconica/Getty (l), Nick White/Taxi/Getty (c), Chris Clinton/Photonica/ Getty (r); **2:** Michael Hemsley; **3:** Michael Hemsley (c), Jack Flash/Stone/Getty (b); **5:** C. Devan/zefa/Corbis; **7:** Peter Cade/Iconica/Getty; **8:** ColourBlind Images/Iconica/Getty (l), VCL/Chris Ryan/Taxi/Getty (cl), Michael Hemsley (cr), Julien Capmeil/Photonica/Getty (r); **13:** Shaun Egan/Stone/Getty; **14:** Martin Ruetschi/epa/Corbis; **22:** Alan Schein Photography/Corbis; **31:** Martin Ruetschi/epa/Corbis; **35:** Mauro Speziale/Photonica/Getty; **39:** Rob Melnychuk/ Digital Vision/Getty; **44:** Justin Pumfrey/Taxi/Getty; **51:** Stewart Cohen/ Photographer's Choice/Getty; **53:** ColourBlind Images/Iconica/Getty; **57:** Nick White/ Taxi/Getty; **59:** VCL/Chris Ryan/Taxi/Getty; **67:** Jerome Tisne/Iconica/Getty; **68:** Stuart O'Sullivan/The Image Bank/Getty; **70:** Kaz Mori/Photographer's Choice/Getty; **75:** Chris Clinton/Photonica/Getty; **76:** Ryanstock/Taxi/Getty; **79:** Michael Hemsley; **83:** Sharon Wharton/Workbook Stock/Getty; **92:** Michael Hemsley; **101:** Ryanstock/ Taxi/Getty; **103:** Michael Hemsley; **106:** Julien Capmeil/Photonica/Getty; **110:** Jack Flash/Stone/Getty; **112:** Michael Hemsley.

All other images © Dorling Kindersley.

For further information see www.dkimages.com

Authors' acknowledgments

I would like to thank Dr Susan Michie of the Centre for Outcomes Research and Effectiveness, Department of Psychology, University College London for her help with this book, and Rachel and Alex Manktelow, for just being great

Authors' biographies

James Manktelow is CEO of MindTools.com, the Internet's most visited career skills resource. Prior to MindTools, James' career spanned strategic analysis, business development, marketing, production and project management, business analysis, and consultancy for major corporations in most European countries. He has led teams at all corporate levels and has worked with others to build two successful companies. He is author of *Mind Tools and Stress Tools*, co-author of *Make Time for Success* and *How to Lead: Discover the Leader Within You*, and author of DK's *Worklife: Time Management*. His home page is at www.jamesmanktelow.com.